"HEART TO HEART"

THE SONG OF TWO NATIONS

WITH

AFTERTONES AND OTHER PIECES

BY

IVAN HUES

LONDON

KEGAN PAUL, TRENCH & CO., 1, PATERNOSTER SQUARE

1889

"HEART TO HEART"

AND OTHER PIECES

"I must say that I am much and favourably impressed by the wealth of imagination and the descriptive power of the poem. There are whole passages of very considerable excellence, many in Canto III., and many in Canto VI. especially. The lyrics are very sweet and spontaneous, and show a good ear; while the ease of the rhymes, many of them double rhymes, is very remarkable."— LEWIS MORRIS.

TO

THE MILLIONS

WHO ARE DEEPLY INTERESTED

IN THE OBJECT WITH WHICH IT IS WRITTEN,

THIS BOOK IS DEDICATED

BY

THE AUTHOR.

CONTENTS.

———◦◦◦———

CANTO FIRST.

B

"HEART TO HEART."

THE SONG OF TWO NATIONS.

———◦◦◦——— ·

CANTO FIRST.

THERE is a time in most men's lives, methinks,
When, crusht by disappointments and reverses,
The baffled soul from worldly contact shrinks,
The heart its sorrows in itself inhearses.
The halo of youth's dreams too soon disperses,
And leaves man faced by stark reality;
Still he his broken idols sternly nurses,
And threads life's mazes sad and silently,
Passing through dreary years in cold misanthropy.

————

Not least I trow with poets is it so, ·
Whose dreams of life are beautiful and bright,
Till blurred, effaced their fervid fancies' glow,
And their ideal world is shattered quite.

Then life is long, blank as oblivion's night ;
But time at last dispels their spirits' gloom,
And frees their fancies for triumphant flight,
While fires of prophecy their souls illume,
And their hearts' dearest hopes sweet song will disentomb.

———

Aneurin I, who, bard and sage and seer,
For many years have been both mute and dark,
My sullen soul strange sounds was prone to hear,
My lightless eyes invisible forms would mark,
And from long watching wan, close care, and cark,
My form is bowed, my lengthened locks are hoar,
My life hath burned to its last lessening spark ;
My flagging feet, full fleet and firm of yore,
Will lightly fall no more on th' earth's green, flowered
    floor.

———

The days have ebbed like waves of time far out
Since silence fell on my dark soul dismayed,
And like some hall where phantoms roam about,
My heart hath rung with chords by dead hands played.
Yet as the swan with bleeding breast self-made,
Trills his death-wail as down the stream he sails,
I sing this song with the last breath delayed,
For every vision of my fancy pales
Before this one which now my raptured brain unvails.

———

The glorious sun is rolling high
Above the blue, mysterious sky,
As dreaming on this lonely shore
I listen to the ocean's roar,
And watch the booming waters roll
In vast unrest from pole to pole,
Their white waves rearing high and bright
Through sunny day and starry night.
Roll on, boom on, remorseful sea,
Till bursts thy bosom's agony!
I know how full and fittingly
Thy moan, and murmur, and sobbing swell
Will blend with that far-sounding song
That floats the mountain mists among,
And the strange tale the Bard must tell.

Beyond the dim horizon's haze
Far sweeps my mystic mental gaze,
And leagues along the ocean's breast
A bright land lifts its gleaming crest,
A fair isle lockt in the sea's embrace,
The home of many a hardy race,
Where women are fair and men are bold,
And cities treasure up wealth untold;
Bold of all bold, free of all free,
Rulers alike on land and sea,

Brave of all brave, fair of all fair,
Blood of the mightiest mingles there.

————

The people's kingdom in the sea,
A lovely island home and free,
I there behold, and wild and grand
Uprise the hills of Cambrian Land,
The whilom home of minstrelsie,
Of music, song, and poetry.

————

How many stirring lays have rung
Those hills, and woods, and vales among;
How many charms of magian lore
Still linger round her temples hoar!
You who would wend in fancy's dreams,
Pursue those bright meandering streams,
Past caves where lost traditions dwell,
Past lichened crags that weirdly tell
Of lone enchantment's faery spell;
You who would muse on noble deeds,
On faded fanes and crumbled creeds,
Their vestiges might still behold
By ford, and pass, and castle old.

————

But hark! across the sobbing sea
What sounds are these that come to me?

I hear a voice that floats afar
In song that falls as from a star ;
I see a youthful wanderer stand
On a blue summit lofty, grand,
From whence man's eye might almost see
The Wiht Land wide from sea to sea.

———

What joy to view that fair domain
Of river, forest, hill, and plain !
With pride the poet's eye is cast
On scenes so varied, fair, and vast ;
But these strange tones my ears that greet,
Now sadly stern, now strangely sweet,
Must deeply stir the listening soul
More than the wandering waves that roll
   Along the shifting, shingly beach,
More than the wintry winds that roar
Along the bleak tempestuous shore,
   Through mountain gorge, or forest reach.

———

One from the Cambrian Land is he
Who tops the Beacon's purple height,
As faintly falls his song to me
As songs are heard in dreams at night.
The tender blue of the western sky
Seems his slight form to magnify

As in its crystal light he stands
Like some celestial form with hands
Outstretched, now claspt, now spread apart,
As one who from a yearning heart,
Half-way 'twixt earth and sky revealed,
To heaven, or earth, or both appealed.

———

And now his glance, as 'twere the last,
Back o'er the Walian Land is cast ;
White shines his open brow and bare,
In glossy gleams his waving hair
Floats darkly on the mountain wind
Towards the path his feet would find.
His mien is calm, his soul upright,
His eye burns with a saddened light,
As if some sorrow smote his heart,
   And anguish held his brain in spell,
And made the tear of shame upstart,
   And patriotic pride upwell.

———

Oh, hear the beardless bard's appeal
Who're wise to watch the Wiht Land's weal,
For strong though sensitive the mind
Whose song rides on the mountain wind :

———

"O Land of wild and wondrous hills !
Dear land of valleys green and fair !
Deep sorrow now my bosom fills,
As from your presence in despair
I tear myself, perhaps no more
To see those lofty mountains rise
In grandeur from the golden shore,
To pierce the clouds and kiss the skies.
Would that my lips a song might frame
To kindle in those hearts a flame,
The hearts of all your people there,
The hearts of all your bardic sons,
The hearts of all your daughters fair,
The hearts of even your humblest ones,
From isolation's depths to claim,
And light them up the heights of fame !

"Would that my voice might once awaken
The sounds that in their souls seem dead !
Would that my music-thirst were slaken
In their deep founts of song unshed !
Would that my tongue might once deliver
The message which my heart would send !
A song should flow then like a river
That broadens as it nears the end—

That grows more deep, more strong, and ever
To seaward rolls resistlessly
To swell the long profound endeavour
That sways the overwhelming sea.
So should my parting song, increasing
In volume and in depth, outflow
Till, surging o'er their hearts unceasing
Its meaning they perforce would know.

———

" But 'tis in vain the heart so yearns,
And 'tis in vain the soul so burns
For power divine of heart or hand.
So fare you well, O Cambrian Land !
Farewell, farewell, though once again
I turn to view your wild domain,
And with a long, last, lingering gaze
Fix memories time shall ne'er erase

———

" Here on the Borderland I stand,
Athwart the line proscribed of yore,
When Offa with his ruthless band
Made the great Dyke and fiercely swore
The Waal who dared to cross it died
By his unchangeable command,
My face turned to the Mountain Land,
My back to broad Sabrina's tide,

And well I know where'er I tread
Is holy and historic ground,
And heroes through long ages dead
Are moving shadowless around.

———

"Swift through my brain all thick and fast
Crowd visions of the perished past.
Remote and near and all around
On every inch of this fair ground,
I see the hosts again engaged
In fiercest wars for ages waged;
The air is filled with battle sounds
And rent as was their flesh with wounds;
Now near, now far, now high, now low,
This way and that the noises go,
Along the hills the clamours roll,
Dark grows the sky, and dark my soul.

———

" I'll see no more!   My senses swim,
My heart grows faint, my eyes grow dim;
  Pass from my view, too dreadful scene !
Back to your rest, fierce phantom hordes,
Nor more renew with phantom swords
  The barbarous struggles that have been !
They were of old the Wiht Land race,
And Britons still may proudly trace

Descent from such brave ancestry ;
But dark those ages were, and all
Rejoice they fade beyond recall
   In mists of dim antiquity.
They were in bout and battle bold
And braved the fiercest foe to hold,
   The sea-locked homes they loved so well.
Green as their island be their fame,
And beacon-like blaze every name,
   In the Island story sages tell.
The Indian, true, hath fallen too,
The Arab, Chinaman, Hindoo,
The Kaffir, Maori, and the Moor ;
There is no land but hath a plain
Where countless myriads have been slain
   To keep invaders off its shore.
But never yet it shall be said
A minstrel's soul was dull or dead
   To love of native land or kind,
For he who frames his tender lays
To sing in Love's and Virtue's praise
   No unlamented fate would find.
He who the Patriot's power would sing,
And make his harp with fervour ring,
   Extolling noble, knightly deeds,
Himself desires affection's tear
And Honour's voice above his bier,
   And Love's remembrance needs.

" Then say not Awen turned his back
Upon the Cambrian Land for lack
Of soul the generous joy to feel
That binds him to her woe and weal.
Fair Cambria ! though wild and free,
Deep stirs my heart with love for thee,
And high my soul would soar to claim
Full measure of your ancient fame,
And for your future glory make
Life's proudest efforts for your sake.

" Land of the Waal ! in Heathenesse
Misnamed with Hate's blind bitterness !
Land of true Briton ! chosen home
Of mighty souls imperious Rome
Who dared defy !   Proud Walian land !
Too feeble is my halting hand
To paint your beauty, grandeur, grace,
Or your long history to trace.

" Not mine the task, though mine the will,
To sing your charms with fitting skill.
I feel the joy, I feel the spell,
But lack the power divine to tell.
Some master will, with holy fire,
For such high theme attune his lyre ;

But none can more admire than he
Who in his heart sings secretly."

—————

The singer paused, and on his breast
Enclaspt his hands as if impressed
With some unfathomable thought;
And all his being was strangely wrought
With deep, intense, and fervid feeling.
Athwart his busy brain came stealing
His life's young memories.   Then higher
His voice rose : "None can more admire
Than he who sings to you, O land
Of bright and ever-varied scene,
Now wild and weird, majestic, grand,
Now peaceful, picturesque, serene.

—————

Oh, be it in its summer's mildness
    With balmy breezes soft and warm,
Or in the dreadful winter's wildness
    With bleaching cold or blinding storm.
In the springtime, in the autumn, in the bloom and in
    the sere,
In the mingled mellow glories ever changing through the
    year,
Thou to me art ever charming, ever beautiful and dear."

—————

Again he paused with pose of grace,
And still serener seemed his face.
"Dear land !" he said, "I love you well,
What though I leave you now to dwell
In other lands beneath the sky,
I know not where, I know not why."

Still calm he stood, as one debating
Within himself although decided,
As one a moment contemplating
By some God-given wisdom guided.
Then sweetlier than a lover singer
He said, "I must not longer linger ;
I'll cross the line proscribed of old,
And wander on unchecked and bold,
Until I know the glow and glory
Of that great land most famed in story
Where passed our fathers, proud to know
'Twas theirs, long centuries ago."

The wanderer would have hastened then
Far from the Mountain Land away,
But many memories came again
And held him singing this last lay :
"Farewell, dear land ! for me no more
Spring's flowers will stud your valleys o'er ;

No more your hills with glory shine
As erst when joy and faith were mine ;
No more with unrestrained delights
Shall I ascend your sky-capt heights,
To gaze with raptured soul and free
From ridge to ridge as over a sea
Whose waves, too huge for gods to quell,
Were turned to granite in their swell,
Nor peer into deep glens below
Where rills to stately rivers grow ;
No more stand sheer on highest peak
When night lours or morn's glories break,
Nor struggle down its rugged side
When mists the gaping gorges hide.
Farewell, lake, forest, hill, ravine,
All have my loved companions been.

" No more I'll seek bright meads and green
Deep-bosomed in the fertile vales ;
Nor in the pleasant shades be seen
Of woodlands in the leafy dales ;
Nor wander through cool hazel brakes,
By cornfields seeming golden lakes ;
Where waves of light and shadow pass
Along the nodding, ripening grass ;
Through sunny lanes with flowering charms,
By cosy cots and white-walled farms,

White waterfalls and limpid streams,
Where many a bardic shepherd dreams.

——

" The mountain breeze is sweet to me,
And sweet the mountain heather too,
When comes the summer o'er the sea
With southern skies bright, warm, and blue ;
The mountain ferns are soft and green,
And grand the gorse in golden bloom—
More bright the health-rose there is seen
Than in the crowded city's gloom.
'Tis pleasant on green slopes to lie,
Where leverets freely frisk and play ;
To hear far up the sunny sky
The mountain lark's ecstatic lay.
How blithely sings the mountain rill,
As downward to the vale it flows ;
How blithe the mountain milkmaid's trill,
As lilting to her kine she goes !
The shepherd lad is lithe of limb,
His eye is keen, and bright his look ;
What king would not exchange with him
The sceptre for the hazel crook ?

——

" Let those whom wilder scenes delight
Ascend yon towering Beacon's height,

C

When lowering storm-clouds gather round,
And fierce blasts swoop with deafening sound ;
When rooks and ravens croak with fright,
And madly dash in circling flight,
When jackdaws shriek and curlews cry,
And cleave with might the black'ning sky ;
When hawk and kite their prey forego,
And drop to sheltered cliffs below ;
When bursts the forkèd lightning's blaze
From the Plutonian gloom, and plays
Along the horizon flash on flash,
Tracked by the thunder's boom and crash ;
When pours with roar and rush the rain
As if to flood the world again,
And every rut in the hillside
Sends down the slopes its turbid tide,
And streams which scarce an hour ago
Ran leisurely with limpid flow,
Now surge along their bouldered course
With turgid and tumultuous force,
Till thundering rivers seaward roll
Where late but sluggish streamlets stole ;
When earth and sky commingled seem,
And Chaos reigns again supreme.

———

" But cease, my tongue !   It naught avails
If grand the hills, or green the vales,

If lakes are clear, or streams are bright,
If storm-clouds break on every height,
Or sheds the sun his golden rays
O'er hill and dale and forest ways.

———

" I'll sing no more. No song or chant
Can bring to Cambria her want;
The sweetest song that Bard might sing
No solace to the heart can bring.
      Nay, song is dead,
      The muse hath fled
To some more favoured land afar,
Where brighter skies and seasons are—
Some greener island in some sea
More blue and bright than we can see,
Her meeter home, and comes no more,
Great Land of Shadows, to thy shore.

———

"O Land of mouldering, mystic fame !
Time's dust obliterates thy name,
Thy story, writ as 'twere in sand
Where people pass from sea to land,
Beneath the footprints disappear
Of each succeeding, passing age,
And soon, as tides the sandhills clear,
Oblivion's waves will sweep the page.

———

" Land of the Hills ! no more you boast
Your sacred bards or warrior host,
Nor with recurring hope recall
Their noble rise or grander fall.
Men mark no more song's mystic charms,
Or grace of chivalry or arms.
Yours was the past ; in hoary scrolls
Are graven the names of mighty souls ;
But as the sunken sun still gleams
Behind the hills, when long his beams
Have ceased to cast their golden glow
Into the valley's depths below,
So shines the light of vanished days,
Though none of its resplendent blaze
Now lights the passing poet's path,
Or saves him from the scoffer's wrath.

" Dimmed is the warrior's godlike fame,
Forgotten long the patriot's name,
No more the sounds of minstrel's lyre
The souls of prince and peasant fire ;
Hushed as the voices of their days
Are all the mightiest singers' lays,
The moving strains of heroes sung
In depths of the dead sea are flung
Of all dead sounds.   Ev'n all the band
That fell beneath the unkingly hand

Are mute as his untuneful tongue
Who stemmed with blood their tide of song.

———

" God rest their dust !   No more I may
Tread where their sacred ashes lay ;
Farewell the land that heard their lays
With rapture in primeval days.
Great land, made sacred by their dust
And by their sacred blood, I must
Go hence, but though my outward eyes
Behold you in endearing guise
No more, yet in my brain will live
Your light and joy and loveliness,
Like that supernal face gods give
To poets, but ere they caress
Recall, yet leave its light divine
For ever on their souls to shine,
So all your beauteous scenes and bright
Will light my memory and delight."

———

Then Awen ceased, and wistfully
He turned and gazed towards the sea.
He saw the white ships come and go,
He saw the waters' restless flow ;
He thought of lands where he might stray,
Beyond the billows far away,

While over his searching, saddening eye
Came mists which blended sea and sky ;
He heard the wailing of the wind,
But naught of fear was in his mind.
Oh, men might laugh, and men might sneer,
Still Cambria to him was dear.

CANTO SECOND.

CANTO SECOND.

SWEET World! how soon we learn, and how severely,
That those we often gaze on, seeing clearly,
    Aren't the forms that move before us
      In the open light of day ;
That the singers sweetliest singing, softly singing
And the silver voices ringing, sweetly ringing,
    In our minds, are not the chorus
      That we hark to on our way !
      All the beautifullest faces,
        All the forms of greatest splendour,
      All the voices and the graces,
        That we cherish with a tender
Deep, enduring, and long-mellowing memorie,
Are those only we may never hear or see
With our fleshly eyes and ears, but well we know
In our fancies they will ever come and go,
Loved and loving, with a self-renewing love
That shall grow and rise all other joys above.

———

      The form of that lonely young singer
        Will move evermore in my mind ;

And his song's sad echoes will linger
　　Around as a wandering wind.
Will pause and drop imperceptible wings,
To languish about the neglected strings
Of a harp that wails in its slow decay
For the master hand that has passed away.

———

While still around those tones are ringing,
We may discover who was singing,
And learn why he would choose to wander
From the loved land of mountains yonder,
And why a bard so young and free,
　　In loneliness and mysticy,
Should send o'er mountain, wood, and dell
To his home land his long farewell.

———

To gauge a song's mellifluent flow
And grasp its drift, 'twere well to know
The singer and his life's career—
If bright and smooth, or wild and drear;
If flexile, easy, and serene,
Or fiery, fast, and over-keen,
Like buoyant barque in balmy breeze,
Or crippled craft in wintry seas;
If warm his heart as torrid glow,
Or chill as the perennial snow;

If free his soul for fearless flight,
Or barred and banned by passion's blight.

———

I've heard it as it rolled along
From hill to hill, that lonely song,
And I no mystic were forsooth
Heard I without both wrath and ruth,
And I no worthy seer could be
Did I not wot, and painfully,
The secret of that wanderer's woes,
And why from Cambrian Land he goes.

———

Ah! clear and plainly I have seen,
And plain and clearly I foresee,
What Awen's opening life hath been,
And what its fateful close will be.
Such are the secrets I would tell,
And they will hear who deem it well,
And they will pass unheeding by
Who love not gentle poesy.

———

But I must sing as I must see,
Sweet mystic power vouchsafed to me!
And I will sing as I have seen,
Without apology, serene,

Without excuse, without parade,
The truths of time to me conveyed.

———

Came Awen of a knightly race,
And lengthy lineage well might boast
Were he of those who love to trace
Their coming from a lordly host,
And to themselves would arrogate
The fame of the forgotten great.
Great bards, and chiefs, and men of might
That long and lofty line did light,
And legends of most stirring note
Were sung of them in times remote.

———

Syr Morlaes crossed the seas afar,
Where fell the moon with the evening star,
And filled his ships with many a prize
That dazzled the boldest 'venturer's eyes ;
Many strange peoples spoke his fame,
And tyrants feared to hear his name.
Syr Uvane laid beneath the wave
Which ninth in the roll of the waters swept,
Many a Viking low in his grave
Ere on the shore his boat's keel leapt.
Gadreve the Bold in many a fight
Had quelled his foes with matchless might ;

And Murien's brows were bound with bays
For wondrous lore and deathless lays.

———

Though long ago dread war's alarms
Had ceased to summon the chiefs to arms,
And feud and foray waned and passed,
As fiercest storms abate at last,
Within those walls where Awen Childe
Beside his sire's grim frowning smiled,
The semblance of that age gone by
Still awed the hapless wanderer's eye.

———

Yet few the wanderers are, I know,
That by the Towers of Dynver go,
For lonely loom they grim and grey,
As brooding o'er their own decay
On yonder black and beetling rock
    Which frowns upon the sea beneath,
Against whose base, with endless shock,
    The breakers surge, and swirl, and seethe.

———

Behind them wooded uplands rise,
And hills whose blue tops touch the skies,
While Dynver Vale lies fair below,
With hosts of brightest flowers aglow ;

The air with music throbs and swells
From fragrant groves and scented dells.

———

Upon that storm-struck headland height
Oped Awen's eyes first to the light,
But hushed the wind, the sea was still,
And bright the sun o'er vale and hill ;
The woods were fresh with summer showers,
The meadows gleamed with clust'ring flowers ;
On all the plains, the hills, the woods,
Smiled Nature in her happiest moods,
And Dynver Towers within, without,
Resounded with the festal rout.

———

Syr Utar, Lord of Dynver Towers,
Bethought him of ancestral powers,
And ancient customs, many a one,
Long handed down from sire to son.
He summoned then the motley band
Who wrought his will and tilled his land,
And bade them gather in banquet-hall
To hold with him high festival.
So came each one in his degree,
And formed a jocund company.
Then when the feast was fully sped,
Syr Utar, seated at the head,

Bade all fill up their beakers high,
And swift together drain them dry.

Thus pledging deep the welcome heir
Born to his house that morning fair,
"'Tis meet," he said, " the sun should shine
Bright on the birth of son of mine—
Full meet the scion of a race
Of chiefs of might and knights of grace,
Th' earth in her gayest garb should greet
With flowers around his rosy feet ;
Meet, too, that we the glad event
Should mark with feast and merriment,
So pledge him deep and pledge him long,
Let mellow mead and brown ale strong
Flow freely round, and let the day
Bring graceful speech and stirring lay."

Syr Utar raised his foaming cup,
And every bowl went flashing up,
And brimming tankards all around
Together clashed with cheering sound.
The while each guest erect upsprang,
And with brave cheers all Dynver rang,
And lusty greetings high and higher
For helpless babe and potent sire,

Then all with simultaneous draught
The mellow mead and strong ale quaft.

———

Thus had it been in Dynver Tower
Since Dynver was a place of power,
And well had each succeeding chief   .
Held that old custom dear and lief,
And in his turn thus every one
Pledged with his train his firstborn son ;
And like his sires, all brave and wise,
Utar assumed the chieftain's guise,
And proud his heart within him burned,
Deeming old times again returned.

———

Sooth, had he been a prince that day,
As sooth he was by blood, men said,
No knightlier could have been his sway,
Nor nobler his antique display.
Full ample was the feast he spread,
Full jocund the carouse he led,
And frequent were the quips and jests
With which he cheered his boisterous guests,
And song and toast and sentiment
Around the tables freely went.

———

Anon a bard who occupied
The seat of fame at Utar's side,

And silent sat, turned to accost
A serving youth behind the host,
And straightway at his feet was placed
The harp that many a feast had graced.
Right well they knew that harp, and he
Who conjured forth its melody
Full oft had made old Dynver Tower
Resound with lays of grace and power.
In sooth, in that same grim abode
He sang Syr Utar's birthday ode,
And now in somewhat altered strain
Proud Dynver's heir he'd sing again.
Oh, joyously the companie
Await the thrilling symphony !

The honoured bard, old Ian Dhare,
Attuned the triple strings with care ;
But there was a strangeness in his touch
Which puzzled the anxious gathering much.
The lustre of his deep, dark eye
Betrayed some dream-drawn prophecy ;
And when, the mystic prelude over,
The poet's voice began to hover
Above the harp's mysterious swell,
The guests were seized as by a spell
And marvelling listened, yet passionately
Drank the unwonted minstrelsy,

D

While the haughty host with marked dismay
Watched the procedure of the lay.

IAN'S SONG.

Elate was the heart of the man with pride
Who bore to his castle a lovely bride ;
But the soul of the knight was crushed with shame
Whose lady played wanton with Virtue's name.

———

Radiant and flushed as a summer morn
Was the noble to whom an heir was born ;
But the patriot sire was bowed with woe
Whose son from the land of his birth would go.

———

Drink to the noble, the patriot sire,
The knight, and the man with his heart on fire ;
Though bitter their sorrow and shame, they come,
Death, sorrow, or shame, to every home.

———

Death and dark Sorrow went journeying out,
White Death said to Sorrow, " Be thou my scout.
Go forward to castle and cot and see
If peasant or prince be ready for me."

———

And Sorrow went forward, filling with gloom
Castle and cot, and the darkness of doom.

Death followed soon after and chose his prey,
And peasant nor prince dared say to him nay.

———

But nothing with sorrow or shame have we,
Sweet life new-given, not death we see ;
So drink to the father and drink to the son,
And length to the life that has just begun.

———

I've feasted before and drunken the wine,
Singing the birth of the last of the line,
Joy to thee, Dynver, and joy to thy heir,
The morn of whose life is cloudless and fair.

———

Toss the tankards again, drink deep, drink long,
The mead is right mellow, the ale is strong ;
A poet had visions he could not disclose,
And a young man's friends were an old man's foes.

———

A babe was born in luxurious bed,
A youth on the verge of a cliff lay dead ;
The infant was rocked in a gilded cot,
But the dead youth even a grave had not.

———

Drink to Syr Utar, and drink to his son ;
One life begins when the other is done.

Sweet babes ! ye are born, but 'tis men who die,
And each one works out his own destiny.

———

Bard Ian ceased, and every guest
With some vague presage seemed impressed,
And though they loved the poet well,
And oft had owned the magic spell
With which he bound their hearts, yet now
No form of praise could they bestow
With look, or sign, or hand, or tongue—
No recognition of his song,
But only gazed as each would say,
" What means old Ian's random lay ? "

———

Uprose Syr Utar, proud and fierce,
    And scanned the tables down,
His gaze seemed every mind to pierce
    And make its thoughts his own ;
His eye, erst while glad, clear, and bright,
Now gleamed with stern imperious light ;
His firm-set form, from crown to heel,
A kingly rage seemed to reveal ;
But " Drink !" was all he said, and laught,
And drained his goblet at a draught.

———

Recalled to a sense of fealty,
The guests upsprang right readily,

And tossed their beakers high again ;
They drank to Utar deep and long
In mellow mead and brown ale strong,
And cheered their host in lusty vein ;
Ian the bard drank deeply too,
But drank in silence, and withdrew.

———

Though bravely for a time suppressed,
Wild passions warred in Utar's breast,
And frequently there fiercely flashed
From his dark eyes all deeply lashed
Gleams which betrayed the fire within,
As lightnings glancing up the sky
Proclaim the tempest hovering nigh
Before the thunder peals begin.
So when again Syr Utar spake,
His voice, as distant thunders break,
Low murmured down the room,
And first he said in accents fair,
" Long I have loved thee, Ian Dhare,
In sunshine and in gloom,
And shall the tenor of a song
Destroy the love hath lived so long ?
Nay, nay ; 'twas but the poet's whim,
And we no blame can fix on him

Who sings but as he musing may
His random, strange, unbidden lay."

———

Then came the tempest gradually.
" 'Twas but thine eccentricity,
O Ian Dhare, and whiles they live
Such is the bards' prerogative;
But mark you all beneath this roof,
If in this world there should be proof
That in this song there has been aught
Of inspiration—something caught
From the all-knowing gods, and it should pass
That he hath seen the future in the glass
Of prescience—— But no, I will not think
It can be.   Out, false fancies !   Drink !
Utar to Ian drinks, to mirth,
And to the land that gave him birth ! "

———

Not loth drank all the guests, and deep,
As if each reveller strove to steep
His brain in the Lethean draught;
But mead and ale in vain they quaft;
No Bacchanalian spell yet known
Remembrance of that strain could drown.
Throughout the revel Utar's mind
To dread, foreboding thoughts inclined.

" If it ever come to pass," said he,
" That Dynver's heir can faithless be
To the traditions of his race,
Let him be cursed!   And may disgrace
Deep and enduring, death and hell,
Be theirs who by foul means and fell
Win him to alien ways !   Deep hate
And quenchless we'd perpetuate
In his breast, as in ours, for those
Who are our race's natural foes.
'Tis our inheritance, to run
Without surcease from sire to son."

The guests applauded, and upstood
Defiant, while in fiercer mood
The host said on, " May Heaven disown
All aliens !   In our Isle were known
No Waal Land save for them, and we
Were Britons still from sea to sea."

The feast had past, and long again
Did peace over Dynver Towers reign,
And of the parted guests not all
Would gather again in banquet-hall.

Through storm and calm, sunshine and showers,
The seasons rolled over Dynver Towers,

And Dynver's heir, through smiles and tears,
Grew gently with the passing years.
But I need linger not or dwell
On his white babyhood, or tell
How he through rosy childhood passed;
He was a boy of thoughtful mood,
And loved the woodland solitude,
The lonely mountains high and vast.
Syr Utar with misgiving saw
Him view the sea's expanse with awe,
With wonder the unbounded sky.
The vulgar said his wits were weak,
The rustics deemed him wise and meek,
And in green elfin ring to die.
Thus superstition ever regards
The stripling who too soon discards
    The tricks and toys of infancy,
And takes to reading ponderous books,
And wandering on the banks of brooks
    That roam and sing incessantly.
But the revolving years, which wrought
Sweet changes in the child, had brought
    Many a dreary change around:
The mother who with pride and joy
And tender love had watched the boy,
    Was laid in the green churchyard ground.
That was a crushing grief to bear
Both for Syr Utar and his heir;

But Utar, while the years would bring
To Awen all life's balm and spring,
Felt winter's snows upon him fall.
So, bending age and grief withal,
He seldom passed from Dynver's hall,
At morn or noon or evening fall,
And in his gloom that birthday song
But seldom rose his thoughts among.
Ian the Bard for many a day
His earthly harp had ceased to play.

———

Sorrow and Death at Dynver had been
   Unwelcome visitors and unkind,
And beautiful forms no more were seen
   In the deep gloom they left behind.
And, of their light and love bereft,
The Childe to lonely ways was left;
So he was wont at times to roam
In secret from his darkened home.
But year by year, as time sped on,
In gentleness of soul he shone,
In comeliness of person, too,
And nobleness of mind he grew,
For Nature with unerring hand
His mind and body sweetly planned,

And marked their meet development
As through her wonder-world he went.

He loved the Mountain Land full well,
And knew each hill and wood and dell,
Each lake and stream and cataract,
Fair forest glade and flowery tract,
Each pass and cairn and craggy crest
From Severn to the farthest west.

It was an awful joy to him
Along a mountain height to skim,
When shrouding mists enveloped it,
And he through cloudland seemed to flit.
The highest peaks alone he scaled,
As broke the dawn or twilight paled,
And when below deep thunders crashed,
Rolled lurid clouds and lightnings flashed,
He viewed the storm with reverent eye,
Bare-browed against a cloudless sky.

Up many a rugged steep he crept,
O'er which cold, clinging vapours swept,
But on whose heights, unseen below,
He knew the sun did warmly glow,
And he should look on depths profound—
A sea of mists without a sound

Roll on its vaporous waves and break
In filmy spray o'er many a peak,
And all the land, save where he stood,
Submerged beneath a second Flood.

———

Through Nature's wonder-world away
He wandered freely day by day,
And if she wept or if she smiled,
Looked bright and calm, or dark and wild,
For him each mood a charm possessed,
And found its chord within his breast,
And her untold communities
Of birds, and flowers, and plants, and trees,
Of hills, and woods, and lakes, and streams,
Gave to his mind its sweetest dreams.

———

The dreams of boyhood, while they last,
Are beautiful, but all too fast
Time changes brings in long array,
And life less charming seems each day.
Then knowledge comes, and with it joy
Comes only with increased alloy.
So Awen, as the years rolled on,
Felt that with each some hope was gone,
And knowledge came, alas ! that brought
Strange bitterness to sweetest thought,

And to the lowest depths would stir
The soul of the lone wanderer.

———

Some waters will but fiercer make
The thirst which those who drink would slake,
   Yet still they thirsting drink ;
And so men crave forbidden lore,
Which but creates desire for more,
   Though from its pains they shrink.
Even Awen, wandering, knowledge gained
That bitterly his bosom pained,
Yet further, ever further still,
He went through vale and over hill,
And o'er the level lands would stray,
That owned the ancient Islesmen's sway
Ere they, of homes and rights despoiled,
Before the Roman hosts recoiled.
Ah ! is it thought of them that throws
That deepening shadow o'er his brows ?
Fled is sweet joyance, but his mind
Some solace still in thought will find.

———

No bard had sung in Cymric Land
Whose song to Awen was not known,
No harp was struck by master hand
But he had caught its subtlest tone,

Voice ruled no realm of music and
Found not its echo in his own.
He knew that song was ever young,
He knew sweet song could never die—
Knew music thrilled in every tongue
Through every land beneath the sky,
And in his brain sweet sounds had rung
Which rose not west of winding Wye.

Above all sounds all sweet to hear,
Where'er he went in shine or shade,
One voice was sweetest to his ear,
And his quick spirit strongest swayed,
One form in fancy would appear
More bright than loveliest mountain maid.
The form was one of alien mould
In the far reach of fancy shown,
The sounds in alien accents rolled,
The voice was alien in its tone :
Would that in life he could behold
That form and deem it all his own !

As one, while listening to the strain
Poured from the throstle's mellow throat,
Is raptured by a loftier reign
Of music of sublimer note,

And all his soul goes out again
With that mad melody to float,
As higher in the blue domain
The singer soars unseen, remote ;
So Awen heard the tones sublime
Of lofty song above the chime
Of homely minstrelsy that round
Him fluttered with familiar sound,
But like the cloud-enveloped bird,
Unseen the singer whom he heard.

One morn before the summer sun
Far on his golden course had run,
Childe Awen gained the favourite bower
Where he was wont through many an hour
To soothe his soul with melodies
Which unpremeditated rise,
And there, with voice and harp tones blent,
So sweet a strain abroad he sent
That bird and beast with quickened ear
Drew nigh and stood the song to hear.

Those sounds I may not reproduce,
Such tone of harp, such charm of voice,
The gods grant not an old recluse
His darkening spirit to rejoice ;

But I may yet the theme recall,
And something of the form withal :—

———

The saffron morn o'erleaps the hills
  Down to the restless sea ;
The lark upsprings from earth and fills
  The heavens with his glee ;
The sky above, the earth below,
  The sea that rolls between,
Are radiant with a grander glow
  Than ever erst was seen ;
Yet than the earth and sea more fair,
  And brighter than the sky,
Her snowy brow and golden hair,
  Her blue and placid eye.
There is a form of perfect mould,
  A face divinely sweet,
A voice that every sense will hold
  In rapture all complete.
All blooms beside the Queenly Rose
  With lessened lustre gleam ;
The glory of the stars all goes
  Before the Moon's full beam ;
The beauty of the Moon grows less
  When comes the brilliant sun ;

But all things grow in loveliness
　　Where moves that lovely one.

The breezes passing by the bower .
Light-winged flew on to Utar's tower
And whispered in his knightly ear
Some sound it stirred his soul to hear.
His stolid henchman, Garif Grim,
Was summoned hastily to him.
With such unwonted eagerness
Syr Utar for Childe Awen asked,
That Garif in his quick distress
Said in the morning sun he basked.
"Go, Garif, go! and speedily
Bring here," he said, "the boy to me.
I fear of late I do not trace
That light of joyance in his face
That should illume the lineless brow
Of one with hopeful youth aglow."

"If loyal service gave me leave
To speak the thing I deeply grieve
To think," old Garif faltering said.
"Thou halt," Syr Utar cried, "whose head
Hath whitened in these Towers?　Thou,
More privileged than all we know?"

" Then length of servitude must be
For boldness now apology,"
Said Garif hesitatingly ;
" But I would ask with deep respect
If thou dost not too much neglect
Thy gentle heir ? Of late he hath
By many a strange and 'wildering path
Sought company where loneliness
Is mostly found, if one possess
No mind well disciplined, or soul
Held piously in stern control.
I've marked him pace the shoreward walk
When only guilty ghosts should stalk
Abroad to fill the depths of night
With wails the stoutest hearts to fright ;
Have heard his lonely steps recede
From Dynver with unwonted speed
At all unearthly hours, in haste
With the pale dawn to be retraced.
Pale too was he. His eyes, as keen
As yon brown hawk's, at times are seen
To flash with wondrous light, yet nought
Around him could that blaze have brought.
At times they seem to hold in view
All things in earth and sea and skies ;
At others, round and blank and blue,
There's nought they deign to recognize—

E

Not even the lord of Dynver, or
Old Dynver's ancient servitor.
Oft voiceless motions of his lips
Betray occult companionships,
And communings with things that dwell
In the air, unseen, intangible.
Methinks more fleshly company
More welcome to the boy should be."

———

Syr Utar was to anger moved,
For hard old Garif's sayings proved,
Yet chided not, but urged "I would
Speak with the boy and mark his mood.
Thou know'st the mind of youth is aye
Prone to strange fancies.   Haste, away!"

———

So Garif went, and Utar rued
The long years passed in solitude.
"Some mourn the dead," he said, "so long
The living feel neglect and wrong.
What sounds are these that seem remote,
Yet in my burning brain do float?
The song of Ian Dhare!   That song,
Like the bard's tongue, death-husht so long!
How strange the voices of the dead
Come to us when long years have sped!

Haste, Garif ! Wherefore such delay ?
My heart yearns for the boy to-day."

———

Alas, Syr Utar ! and it might
Yearn for him long through day and night.
Keen is old Garif's search, but vain ;
You ne'er may meet the Childe again.
Let Dynver ring with your alarms,
The mountains echo with thy cries ;
Rouse followers in pursuit in swarms,
The wide world of thy loss apprise ;
But ere the fate of Dynver's heir,
By white lips whispering is told,
The lord of Dynver's form will fare   ·
To mingle with the mountain mould,

———

There was but one in Dynver's Tower
Who knew of Awen's favoured bower,
And she had heard that strain full well,
And to his side as by a spell
Was drawn.   With quick and noiseless tread
Through many a leafy maze she sped,
   Like a shaft of light
   That leaves no trace
   Of its sudden flight
   Or its hiding-place,

And in a reverie deep she found
The minstrel, with his arms around
His harp, the triple strings of which
Did still the morning air enrich
With softened sounds, although each finger
Still on the last-struck chord did linger
Irresolute, as if awaiting
The issues of some deep debating
Within his soul.   His back-thrown brow
She lightly kiss'd, and whispered how,
To admit the sun and air, she threw
Her casement open, and in there flew
A sweet, strange bird, whose plaintive note
Welled from gold beak and dappled throat,
As 'twere on fateful mission sent.
How forth anon it warbling went,
Its plumage, purple, gold, and white,
And glossy, glistening in its flight,
A thing all melody and light.
How, watching, listening, then no bird
But her own minstrel's song she heard,
And how she hastened to him.   While
She thus spoke on, her voice and smile
Awakened him, and turned the theme
Of his far fancies and rapt dream.

———

She claspt his hand, and Awen knew
The soft embrace, and to him drew
The fair form, ere he dropt his eyes
From that far realm of phantasies
And fairy scenes on which they dwelt.

———

Close at his side Gladysa knelt,
And gazed up in his face, her own
Lit with the sweet light he had known
And loved from childhood up.　Deep-loved
She was at Dynver, and had proved
To him friend, guide, and sister dear.

———

She was the older, many a year,
And since the day of woe when passed
The Lady of Dynver to her last
Long sleep and silent place of rest
Under the dark yews on the breast
Of yon green upland, she had warmed
With deep affection, and performed
Towards him, with brave and watchful heart,
The mother's and the sister's part.
She thought him still a child, but one
Whose thoughts beyond his years had run.
Chiding yet soothingly she speaks,
As mother to a child who breaks

The bonds of gentle rule, yet feels
She with no rebel spirit deals.

————

She seeks to exercise again
The power that ruled his childhood, when
With a deep prescient joy she watched
Each turn of eye and hand, and snatched
All timely moments to incite
His mind to noblest thoughts, and light
His brain with wonder, for she guessed
There kindled latent in his breast
That fire to glow, if gently fanned,
To light and lead the Cambrian Land.
Oft when he silent sat, she broke
Upon his solitude, and spoke
Of bards and warriors, for good store
Had she of legendary lore,
And he was charmed, amazed, affrighted,
O'erjoyed, dismayed, aroused, delighted.

————

Her hope is gone with her control,
She sways no more that soaring soul;
He heeds no more her legends old,
Of minstrel, bard, or chieftain bold.
He only answers, " Gone are they,
With power of lore and lance and lay."

————

Gladysa pressed Childe Awen's head
Against her troubled heart, and said,
While tears welled in her glistening eyes,
" I know my brother early wise,
But why so rapt and seeming sad ?—
He who has been as gay and glad
And sprightly as the sunny beam
That danced on Ithon's laughing stream ? "

" As transient as that fitful beam
Have been," he said, " my joy and dream."

" How so," Gladysa asked, " your life,
So free from toil and care and strife ?
Your ways have known no check, and bold
And beautiful have been.　Behold
The world's magnificence !　What forms
Of beauty and of grandeur storms
And sunshine make and mar, yet leave
Naught beautiless the eyes perceive !
How bright the sun this morn ! how blue
The sky, and green the land !　All through
The woods, and o'er the heathery hills,
Crags, peaks, and rivers, lakes and rills,
There's loveliness !　All still invite
Your wandering feet ; but, lo ! the light

Seems faded in your eyes; the red
Health-roses in your cheeks seem dead;
Your white brow heavy is with thought,
As one dejected or distressed.
How shall I gather what hath wrought
This change in you?   Your silent breast
Some cankering secret seems to hide.
You love!"

———

"Yes," frankly he replied;
"I love, 'tis true.   Oh, love forlorn!
And many men regard with scorn
My love, alas! and her sweet name
Hold up to ridicule!"

———

"Oh, shame!"
Gladysa cried.   "What can this mean?
Who is your love?   How have you been
Befooled?   What witchery or art
Has lured and snared your boyish heart?
Some wicked, winsome one!   A face
Without a heart!   Oh, shall disgrace——"

———

"Gladysa, nay.   Your overhaste
Befools your judgment; not disgraced—
The gods forbid!—am I or you.
Still true, my sister, all too true

Is that which I have spoken.   Yet
Hear me until I've done, and let
Your heart be patient ; stay your tears,
And you shall know my tale—my fears,
My love, my disappointments ; yea,
My hopes, though few, alack ! are they.
Yes, I have loved, still love, and deep
And true the love I bear, but weep
To find her whom I love a mark
For jest and jeer and jibe ; and, hark !
Her sons and daughters, sore misguided,
Are scoffed at, laughed at, and derided."

———

" Awen ! what must I understand ?
You love———"

———

" I love my native land ! "

———

" Your native land ! " the maid exclaimed,
" That land so old and nobly famed ?
Is it a virtue, then, become
To love the land that is one's home ?
Is it a mark of rarest worth
To love the country of our birth ?
Or is it, you great gods ! now deemed
A crime to hold this land esteemed ? "

———

"I know not, sister, but I dare
To think it is a virtue rare
In men to love that place on earth
Which cannot claim, whate'er its worth,
The honour of his boasted birth.
Else could there be in Britain's Isle
A land which alien hordes revile,
And those who hold it lief and dear
Be held as marks for taunt and sneer?"

"If so, forsooth, foul taunt and sneer
Shall make that land but doubly dear !
Oh, mark you, Childe," Gladysa said,
"You had a mother—she is dead !
You have a sister—she is here !
Lives there the man would dare to sneer
Where Awen was, at her or me,
And lightly pass unscathed and free?"

" He lives not, dares not, sister mine,
For by the names of all who shine
In our Isle's history, I swear
Such meanness from his heart I'd tear
With these weak hands !"

                    " Hands, strong or weak,
Are as the will and spirit to wreak

Redress are roused. Our native land
In light and love alike must stand
As mother dear, whose hallowed name,
Long-cherished rights, and ancient fame
We must uphold, whate'er betide,
With chivalrous and filial pride.
True patriotic fire, I know,
In Awen's soul must ever glow."

———

"A man may love and not possess
The thing he loves, his heart to bless ;
A man may love, yet hold what is
To him no joy or source of bliss.
A knight hath won a maiden's heart,
A king hath grasped that maiden's hand ;
A poet played a patriot's part,
Yet aliens swayed his native land.
Land of the Briton is no more
The Isle of Britain, shore to shore."

———

"The Cambrian Land," said she, "is still
The land we love of vale and hill."

———

"Mountains and valleys ! More," said he—
"Even all this land from sea to sea."

———

"No more," she urged.   " Men seek in vain
For greater in the world's domain.
Yet tell me, Childe, who're they that dare
Deride our land or race, and where
Breathe they unchecked their spiteful sneer
At Cambrian Land so old and dear ? "

———

" 'Twere hard to tell, they so abound
In all the teeming land around,
For with our hills no more we boast
Security against the host
Of rude intruders.   Here they come
And make our Mountain Land their home,
Though they affect sore to despise
Both land and people.   May my eyes
Look on the hosts no more ; my ears
Catch not their levity and jeers.
I will go hence.   Sun, moon, and star
Shall light my wandering way, and far
In some lone land and strange I may
Find Freedom free, and Right in sway."

———

Up rose Childe Awen, and the maid
Sprang to her feet at once, and laid

Her white hands on his arm, as though
She would oppose his going.   So
He drew her to him and embraced
Her tenderly ; then calmly faced
To eastward, and with far-fixed gaze
Piercing the blue horizon's haze,
He said, " Behind that mystic line
The roofs of a world-famed city shine
Under the burning sun.   One day
Through its long busy streets and gay
I wandered, wonderment and awe
And pleasure blent with all I saw.
Anon I strayed to where a crowd
Joined jibe and jeer with laughter loud,
And in their midst, in wrathful mood,
The object of their flouting, stood
A Cambrian Kelt.   My cheek and brow
Flushed with a fierce betraying glow,
And, with strong instinct moved, I would
Defiant at his side have stood.
But scarce was time for act or thought,
Ere by the throat the Cambrian caught
A youth whose gold-fringed lip was curled
With the last sneer that moment hurled.
He seized him with a giant's strength,
And held him fiercely at arm's length.

" How changed the throng ! No more they jeered,
No more they flouted, laughed, or leered,
But, falling back some paces, drew
In circles round the opposing two,
While in the small arena posed,
In ireful fray the assailants closed.
They were a formidable pair,
In golden prime of youth and fair.
The Cambrian, huge of limb and high,
With white teeth set and flashing eye,
Held his fair foe in fearful thrall,
Though he was lusty, lithe, and tall.
Blenched was his cheek, though he would feign
To face the Kelt in braggart vein.
He scowled and laughed contemptuously,
And strove with sudden wrench to free
Himself from that unyielding grip.
In vain ! That grasp he could not slip,
Though he should twist and tug and tear
Till snow-white grew his yellow hair.

"Then hand and foot and knee combined,
Legs interlocked and arms entwined,
The combatants with might and main,
Strove 'vantage grip and trip to gain.
The Cambrian spoke, but who could tell
The fierce words from his lips that fell ?

Though he a score of tongues might prate,
No language then were adequate
His soul's full fury to unbar
But the deep-fired vernacular.
Whatever his words, it seemed his tongue
His arms with double thews had strung,
For swift as thought, as lightning swift,
As sudden gusts tall elms uplift,
Root, bole, and branch, and hurl them prone
On the dank sward with crash and groan,
So swung the Waal from side to side
The wily Cit, who vainly tried
By desperate clutch and agile leap
On the firm ground firm foot to keep.
But, putting forth his utmost might,
The Cambrian drew him above his height,
Then flung him so with piercing yell
Backward amid the crowd he fell.

" With nostrils wide distended, eyes
Flashing fierce fires, huge drops that rise
On strong men's brows when hugely spent
In mighty effort, on his cheeks besprent ;
With hands clenched, and his bare broad chest
Heaving and falling like the unrest

Of yon vast sea, as if distressed
To bound the heart's wild beat, then stood
Erect that rageful form, and viewed
His prone antagonist. The crowd
With oaths and menaces were loud.
But timely through the surging swarm
Pushed one with rough but noble form,
Whose life through many scenes had run,
Whose face was bronzed by storm and sun,
Whose mien was stern, his eye alight
With the proud beam of conscious right.
With saddened voice, but firm and clear,
Half to himself his thoughts expressing,
And half the puzzled crowd addressing,
He said, 'What coward strife is here?
Shame to be such unreasoning fools!
By what authority or rules
May men presume thus to deride
A nation's character or pride?
Why your presumptuous selves embolden
To mock a people grand and olden,
A language beautiful, unique,
 Full of sweet sounds to you unknown,
You who but mangle when you speak
 The mingled tongue you call your own
Oh, cease your ridicule unseemly
Of a bright nation so supremely

Ancient and of lasting fame !
'Tis only ignorance induces
Good men to sink to such abuses,
    Whom wise men pity more than blame.

      ———

"'For me, your taunts and vaunts with scorn
    I hurl again into your face;
Proud of the land where I was born,
    The land of Britain's oldest race.
Yet, from my childhood apt to roam,
    I am a cosmopolitan,
And claim in every land a home
    Where shines the impartial sun on man.
Then sooth a Briton should command
    Free, undisputed right and leave
Throughout the history-hallowed land
    Whose lore his fathers loved to weave.'

      ———

"Then side by side they stood defiant,
As on their might and right reliant.
The silent crowd's averted look
Showed how they felt the staunch rebuke,
But, deigning no reply, they sped
Where'er their divers missions led.

      ———

F

" As stern the cosmopolitan—
Some ancient mariner was he—
Thence piloted the Cymric man
As he would guide a ship at sea."

———

" How nobly said ! how bravely done ! "
Gladysa said ; "and every one
Must honour those who proudly claim
Due reverence for their country's fame."

———

" I am no cosmopolitan,
No ancient mariner," said he,
" But I perceive that every man
Must make himself what he would be.
No honour can be his, or fame,
And none will pay him deference,
Who to the echo of a name
Clings idly and in impotence.
But he who bravely upward climbs,
And leans on no proud ancestry,
Will mark the music of the times,
And make his march in harmony.
No country and no race can give
A man the fame he should desire ;
But each a noble life must live,
To lift the human standard higher.

Each man should live for every man,
And all men live as 'twere for each ;
All men, all nations, the same plan
Should practise zealously and preach."

―――――

" 'Twere very beautiful and right,
But earthly not, nor human quite.
But, hark ! that voice ! 'Tis Garif calls.
They miss us from old Dynver's walls.
Let's haste to them ! " Gladysa sprang
Forward ; the wide wild woodland rang
With her sweet answering voice ; but when
She turned and saw not Awen, then
Her heart beat wildly, and she stood
Like a poor baffled fawn in the wood.
She called on Awen, but no voice
In answer made her heart rejoice.
She hastened to the bower again,
But all her search for him was vain.

―――――

Those secret ways she then retraced,
To Dynver fled in hottest haste,
Like April's nymph, her loosened hair
Streaming along the sun-tinged air,
The tears fast down her white cheeks streaming
Bright in the golden sunbeams gleaming ;

Her looks, but late so bright and warm,
Now cold and clouded with alarm.
And Dynver and the country round
With hurrying feet did soon resound.

The Childe was gone, but to command
One last view of the Cambrian Land,
He sought that lofty height and free
Whence dropt his sweet song down to me,
And from this wave-laved shore again
I sing to you in dreamy vein,
Fast passing world away from me,
The song heard through the sounding sea.

CANTO THIRD.

CANTO THIRD.

THERE is a loneliness in gayest scenes
To that young soul first venturing to roam,
There is a dreariness that intervenes
Darkly between him and his boyhood's home,
No matter how in heaven's blue, cloudless dome
The sun may glow and spread his glories round
From morn till noon, from noon till evening's gloam—
No matter how sweet flowers bestar the ground,
Or the warm air is thrilled with many a pleasing sound.

———

The songs of birds in green, embowered woods,
The low of herds along the scented moor,
The roll of rivers in their varying moods,
And the weird wash of waters on the shore,
The chants of men and women as they pour
Their heart's best feelings out in cherished lays,—
All such glad sounds that joyed his heart before,
Now but sad feelings for the past will raise,
And seem but to forebode ills for remaining days.

———

So Awen felt, as by a route
Trod by no other human foot
From Dynver Towers afar he went,
Filled with a vague presentiment,
And led by some mysterious sway
He knew not how or where away.

———

By unfrequented ways he strode,
Nor touched the dust-white winding road,
But wandered on absorbed, entranced,
Nor marked the way as he advanced;
He heard and saw all things around,
But little heeded sight or sound.

———

He heard the choiring of the birds,
And the soft lowing of the herds;
He heard the buzzing of the bees,
And the weird whispering of the trees;
He heard the revels of the rills,
And the lone echoes of the hills;
He heard the cawing of the rooks,
And the long brawling of the brooks;
He heard the crowing of the cocks,
And the far bleating of the flocks;

He heard the whistle long and shrill,
The shepherd's call from hill to hill,
And the swift sheep-dog's answering bark.

He heard the rumbling of the wains
In the long rugged winding lanes—
Full many pleasant things, but hark !
Sounds grander still than those he hears,
Sounds ever sweet to poet's ears
When bright the sun and warm the air,
And tinged the soul is with despair—
The voices of people who in throngs
Move onward singing choric songs,
Through leafy lanes, by thorpe and fell,
In cool, deep-wooded vale and dell,
Or up some winding path and steep
To where the mountain echoes sleep.

Such were the sounds that faintly first,
Then in a fuller volume burst
Upon the Childe's delighted ears,
As a steep winding way he clears,
And sees behind him fair and grand
The Garden of the Cambrian Land.
And lo ! as though Prometheus clave
Earth half in twain to make a grave

For some dead god, before him oped
A valley long and deep, and sloped
So steeply downward on his side
Its jagged spurs and cliffs defied
Man's foot ; and foaming far below
In the abysmal depths did flow
A surging stream that, sweeping thence,
And tumbling in turgid turbulence,
Down darkened chasms thundering dashed,
Through open forest spaces flashed,
Then white in the wide distance wound
With stately swell to the profound
Sea depths.

There halting on the height
　　That towered between the valleys twain,
He looked about him, and the sight
　　Thrilled him with pleasure and some pain.
It was a scene of great delight,
　　Which he might never see again.
The vale he left with cot and mansion
　　Smiled in the sunshine pleasantly,
Cornfields and grass, a broad expansion
　　Fertile and fruitful and fair to see,
All the green land down to the far grey sea.

While thus he lingered, from the bounds
   Of that deep eastward valley came
Grander and clearer those sweet sounds
   His rapt attention long to claim,
And up the steep on that far side
   He saw the singers slowly climb ;
He heard their chorusing with pride,
   He knew the things they sang sublime.

———

A long and tortuous way they traced,
   Through furze and heath, o'er rock and shale,
And at their head serenely paced
   An elder sage, and white, and hale.
Anon they reached a level ledge
   Midway between the base and brow,
Green and soft-swarded to the edge
   Of cliffs all gloomily that bow
To the white winding floods that rush and roar below.

———

On the green terrace in the side
Of the steep mountain he descried
Green aisles where long quaint-shapèd blocks,
Rough-quarried from adjacent rocks,
Were reared on end in double rows
A mazy passage to enclose,

Up to a double-circled zone
Drawn round a huge grey Rocking Stone.

———

The maze-mouth gained, the elder stood
In mystic and mysterious mood,
As though his spirit communed then
With the hoar shades of antique men.
Meanwhile the motley following
Had ceased their choric song to sing,
And mutely, and with breath abated,
The leader's next commands awaited.
" The summer solstice ! " Awen said,
And to the scene of mystery sped.
Behold the scene !　How vast, how grand !
Superb, sublime on every hand !
A fertile valley from the sea
Winding and narrowing northwardly,
Between eternal hills that rise
Familiar to the eternal skies ;
And from three angles at its head
Three other valleys spring and spread,
Symbolic of the trident she
Wields, mighty ruler of the sea !
And ever from those valleys stream
The marvellous means which make supreme
Britannia wheresoever sweep
The waters of the boundless deep,

And there are swung those Titan hands
That wield and weld the magic wands,
To give our Isle supremacy
Above all other lands that be.

———

Land of the great énchanter !   Mage
Supreme of every land and age !
Ye mystic vales !   In you men view
The footprints of dead Time; in you
Men find the treasures of dead ages ;
You are a book upon whose pages
The world's long history is writ ;
Old Time and new Time meet.   How fit
Are you the world's storehouse to be,
And working place, down to the sea
Sending back that which the dead Past
Saw hidden by the sea in ye,
And locked in your long keeping fast !

———

The sea !   Methinks I hear the boom
Of the Atlantic in each coombe,
And his long roll of mountainous waves
Along those valleys ; hear the caves
Growling unwelcome to each blast,
And the wild hissing breakers cast

Their white bulks in unceasing shocks
On the deep-based and iron-veined rocks.

—————

There still the rocks, the coombes, the caves,
Though there no more the surging waves,
And those bluff cliffs will tower and frown
When æons of new time have flown,
To show new races yet unformed
That Time and all his forces stormed
Round them in vain, and they will be
Proofs of that land's antiquity
Till tides are still, and storms no more
Leave traces on Earth's arid shore.

—————

Mark yonder mass, the Logan Stone !
What centuries of years have flown
Since by some mystic agency
'Twas reared and poised so wondrously
That level granite ledge above
That one man's strength with ease might move,
Or even a simple child might rock
With tiny hands the ponderous block !

—————

Mark, too, how curiously are placed
Those slabs, like gravestones long defaced

Of dead unlettered sculptor's art,
To mark, at intervals apart,
The winding aisles up which are gone
The pageant to the Logan Stone.

The leader halts, the goal is gained,
And every footstep is restrained.
The chief, with grave and solemn mien,
Surveys with kindling eye the scene,
And by him stand, with thoughtful faces,
His followers in their rightful places,
While throng the expectant crowd around,
Now uttering no word or sound.

The sage assumed a robe of white,
A scarf as blue as heaven and bright
O'er the left shoulder threw, and round
His waist a zone of azure wound
And, chanting in sonorous tones,
Moved through the circling aisles of stones
With stately stride, while all his train
With tuneful voices swelled this strain :

THE DRUIDS' CHANT TO THE SUN.

Hail, thou wondrous solar glory !
   Orb of never-changing beam,

Sun of all suns in all heavens,
  Light of every light supreme !
Hail, of all things the beginner,
  Source of life and love and light.
Low we bow before thy presence,
  And do all things in thy sight.

———

Here our fathers owned thy power,
  And this is the path they trod ;
Here as we do now they worshipt,
  Looking up through thee to God.
Thou dost lend the sky its splendour ;
  Thou dost make the oceans roll ;
Thou dost send the seasons over
  All the earth from pole to pole.

———

At thy coming Chaos vanished,
  Far fled Darkness at thy birth ;
Rose divinely nurtured Nature,
  Beauty, grandeur, joy, and mirth.
With thy magic fire impregnate
  Forth unnumbered creatures sprang,
And the world was filled with music
  That throughout creation rang.

———

Hail, transcendent solar glory !
  Orb of never-failing beam,
Wonder of celestial wonders,
  Sun of every sun supreme !
Eye of Light and Source of Being,
  Everything began with thee ;
When thy glory is extinguished,
  Everything will cease to be.

Chorus.

Heart of the universe, shedding
  Warmth for the hearts of us all ;
Soul of the universe, lighting
  Our spirits that rise and fall ;
               Hail, hail !

The chant was over, but hill and dale
Still sounded with the final "hail,"
When high upon the sacred stone
The Elder climbed and stood alone,
Then turned his frenzied eye around,
And silence followed, deep, profound.
His hoary head was bared, his brow
Dome-like, deep-lined, and white as snow,
He then upturned and fixt his gaze
On that unclouded solar blaze,

G

Which he had hailed and silently
Invoked to fire his fantasy;
He with white hair and snowy beard
Some sculptured patriarch appeared.

———

Forth soon his speech began to flow,
First deep, impressive, full and slow,
Then wild, impetuous, like the sweep
Of swoln stream down the mountain steep.
"Hail, brothers, hail," he said.   "We meet
Nature's full fruitfulness to greet,
This hour being the high noon of summer,
And now this earth-called sphere is plumber
With yon high sun than it can be
Through all the year besides, and we
Behold the glories many and great
Which on that sun's warm wooing wait.
How glorious, beautiful, sublime,
This waking after sleeping-time!
How sweet this warm and perfumed breath
After the iciness as of death!
How grand, how wonderful, how strange,
The magical, mysterious change
From winter's dreariness and rigour
To summer's loveliness and vigour;

From bluster, barrenness, and broil
To music, brightness, golden spoil !

———

" All's mystery till we possess
By gift the secret none can guess.
That secret from our seers and sages
Hath been transmitted through long ages,
And still is known, though stranger hordes,
Whose sanguinary and ruthless swords
Are their sole arguments, scoff and sneer
At modern bard and ancient seer.
But heed them not ; 'tis but because
They know not Nature's deeper laws.
Nay, heed them not, contemn and scorn
The sneer of heathenism born,
And view with proud complacency
The glory of our ancestry."

———

The elder paused.　Then, goaded sore
By bitter memories of yore,
Faster his burning words would fall :
" My countrymen !　How shall I call
Forth from your hearts that love and zeal
All for the Cymrik Land should feel?
How shall I rouse within your breasts
That spirit that all too calmly rests ;

How fan within your souls that glow
None but true Britons e'er can know ?

———

" If Saxon, Dane, or Norman be
Among this goodly companie,
Vyvyan, chief bard of Britain, and
Archdruid too of all the land,
I in the Eye of Light proclaim
This Island's oldest creed and fame,
And here defy all scoffs profane
Of Norman, Saxon, or proud Dane !
Oh, let them heed with reverent eye
This lonely place's sanctity !
'Tis holy ground, for let them know
This rock, light-tilted to and fro,
Was reared by olden Islesmen's hands,
And long was known to many lands
Ere heathen Norsemen here were known,
Or Roman arms with conquest shone.

———

" Here walked our ancient sages, versed
In lore so wondrously rehearsed,
That, lured by their unrivalled fame,
From earth's remotest quarters came
High pilgrims hence, on learning bent
The truths of the Omnipotent

By Menw taught in earliest days,
The son of Tergwith of the Rays,
Great fount of mystery and light ;
Here from the gloom of mental night
Were led into the rising rays
Of Wisdom's sun, and the bright ways
Of knowledge ; and so in deep lore learnèd
To divers countries they returnèd,
And spread through many lands full soon
The glories of the mystic Trwn.

―――――――

" Hail, pure, white, heaven-descended Truth,
Beautiful in eternal youth !
Meek Peace, and fair-browed Liberty !
Who strove so manfully for ye
As that calm humanizing band
Who preached forbearance through the land,
And held the truth and right above
All human things, and light and love ?

―――――――

" My brothers of the bardic ring,
Back to those times our fancies wing !
We see the glorious brotherhood
As once on Mona's shore they stood,
In girdled robes of snowy white,
Fit symbols of pure peace and light.

Their songs of praise and hope we hear
Like distant chanting soft and clear.
The fell destroyer's nigh, but lo !
They cease not, and no terrors know,
For sweeter death to them than life,
Must this be brought by mundane strife.

———

"Thrice curst be thou, vile man of Rome !
Who drove them from their sacred home,
And with thy sacrilegious host
Spilled their pure blood on Menai's coast.
Oh, woful day when to thy shore,
Brave Britain, Roman galleys bore
Those eagled legions to despoil
And soak with blood thy cherished soil !

———

"Rouse, brothers ! Can we e'er forget
That in our veins is flowing yet
The strain that fired our fathers' hearts
To deeds of might and noble parts ?
Should we their stainless fame defile
To court the treacherous Norman's smile ?
Should we our ancient rites forego
To please perfidious Saxon foe ;
Or cast aside old rights and rules
To pander to deriding fools ?

Nay ; as long as these old hills uprear
Their heads to clouded skies or clear,
While smile these vales beneath the sun,
And to the seas our rivers run,
Dear to our hearts shall all things be
Passed down from ancient ancestry.
Our grand primeval tongue shall still
Harmonious roll from hill to hill.

———

"Ah, thou didst fail, accursed king,
  To quench with blood the sacred fire ;
The bardic soul shall soar and sing
  In spite of mortal despot's ire !
When princes and dread kings are gone,
  Their names expunged from Time's record,
The sea of song will still roll on,
  And be its own joy and reward."

———

Sage Vyvyan ceased, and loud and long
Rose the wild plaudits of the throng.
Then following in varied strain,
Some minor bards, with might and main,
The enthusiastic groups beguiled
With fervid speech and gesture wild,
And in their cherished pristine tongue
Sweet songs and choruses were sung.

———

Meanwhile a youth with modest mien
Outside the bardic circle's seen.
On a huge rock alone he stands,
And, tokening with uplifted hands,
Essays to speak. In quick surprise
On him are turned a hundred eyes !

Ah, Awen, thy sweet voice alone,
That grace and power, that charm of tone,
That wondrous eye, that lofty brow,
Must win for thee brief hearing now.
But brief 'twill be, so say your say,
As briefly, sweetly as you may.

" Oh, men," said he, " whate'er may be
Our country's pride and history,
All idle are the things you prate.
Why seek you to perpetuate
In these our days, with manner sage,
The foibles of a pagan age ? "

Him with disdain the bards espy ;
A hundred tongues would make reply,
But setting all aside, the chief,
With lofty air and manner brief,
Said, " Who art thou who mak'st so bold
To question Alban customs old ?

This is a time when we rejoice
As did our fathers, and thy voice,
Strange to our ears, but mars the rite,
To us as sacred as heaven's light."

Again the voices of the throng
Were raised in plaudits loud and long ;
But Awen calm, respectful stood,
And added in no wavering mood,
" Arch master of a mystic clan,
I speak but as your fellow-man ;
Or, if it please you better, one
Complaisant as your filial son.
With you I claim the glorious name
Of Briton, and would share the fame
That comes to us still proudly free
Through a long, valiant ancestry.
Reared in the shadows of yon hills,
My bosom ever throbs and thrills
At mention of that name, and far
Be it from me to meanly mar
Observance of their ancient rites.
But can we widen modern rights,
Reviving thus a past so dread
And ways so long effete and dead ;
Dead times of terror, dire distress,
Rapacity, and lawlessness?

Too much bright blood was shed, we know,
Too full the land with wail and woe,
Too many were the feuds and vile
By foemen spread along the Isle,
And better oblivion's veil be cast
For ever over so drear a past."

Deep consternation seized the throng,
Amazement filled the men of song.
But brief the pause that Awen made
Ere mildly he again inveighed :
" Repress your ire, and know me one
Who yields in love of home to none ;
Nor lack I reverence or zeal
For aught enhancing Cambrian weal.
But will it mend our country's state,
Of long past wrongs and ills to prate ;
And shall we swifter progress make,
If we dead grievances uprake ?
Nay, let them rest.　The Past hath sped,
The Future largely looms ahead,
The Present only may we seize
Our country's greatness to increase.
So rouse you, brothers !　Brood no more
O'er things which may have been of yore ;
Let bigotry no longer rule,
To hold you up to ridicule ;

Dispel the superstitious haze
That clouds and shrouds your partial gaze ;
Pause not from Cymrik Land to roam,
And make the whole wide world your home."

Forbear, O youth, nor without need ;
The people's wrath towards thee breed !
See how they sway and surge and press
About thee with no fond caress,
As waves by howling Boreas lasht
Against unyielding rocks are dasht,
And like uncertain winds they veer
'Twixt yell and shout and flattering cheer.

Behold again the master rise
With face austere, and angry eyes
Which on the Childe severely burned
As haughtily he thus returned,
" Oh, traitor-tongued ! too well we feel
No son of Cymrik Land and leal
Could speak as thou dost.   Be content
We heed not thy discouragement.
Naught canst thou say that we should hear ;
Naught gives thee right to interfere
In aught we do.   Nay, thou shouldst know
Time hath not furrowed this bald brow,

Nor on this beard and drooping head
The snows of deepening winter shed,
But something of the world I've seen,
And marked the ways of men, and been
Among them oft.   Whate'er thy birth,
Whate'er thy worth, no land on earth
Can boast an older, nobler race
Than Cambria, and none can trace
A history more great and grand
Than this unmurmuring Mountain Land,
Wild though it be and I for one,
While life is left and yonder sun
Makes bright mine eyes, will proudly dare
To cling to it through foul and fair.
Let alien fools jeer as they will,
Our homes, our loves, our joys are still
Where rise those hills whose bases lie
    Where roll the unfathomable seas,
Whose summits kiss the smiling sky,
    And peer through heaven's veiled mysteries ;
Where valleys green wide spread between
    Enchanted scenes to us supply ;
No other land so grand is seen
    Above the sea, beneath the sky ;
No sight so lovely to our eyes
As this which now around us lies.
Our land and language long shall be
Dear as the light, the air, the sea ;

And dear we'll hold our ancient laws,
Nor brook restraint, nor seek applause."

———

The old man ceased and raised his hand ;
The youth bowed to the stern command.
" The heart goes with you, not the head ;
Let Time be arbiter," he said.

———

Then with more mystic show were ended
The mysteries the sage defended,
And slowly from the scene they went
Along the winding steep descent,
While from the Elder and his train
In volume vast uprose this strain :

———

THE RECESSIONAL.

Old land of our fathers,
Thou art dear to us still,
Each cloud-covered mountain,
Each heather-clad hill.
Each summit that towers
To heaven or near it,
In deepest affection
We hold, and revere it.

———

How grand are the mountains !
How lovely the vales !
The woods are Arcadian,
Elysian the dales.
Our homes are among them,
And ever shall be ;
And proudly we cherish
This land of the free.

———

Still as a statue and as mute
Stood Awen on the rock, each foot
Firm planted, one advanced ; his gaze
Fixt on the long procession's ways
By Vyvyan led ; his ravished ears
Straining at every sound ; his tears
Wetting his whitened cheeks; his breast
Heaving with feelings unsupprest
Beneath his lightly folded arms.
To his rapt soul, what luring charms
Were all those lovely voices, blending
In sweet strains, rapturous, unending !

———

Still with his misty eyes he sweeps
Far down the rugged mountain steeps,
But in the leafy depths below
The bardic train are hidden now,

And their sweet strains, unheard or still,
Wake now no echo in the hill.

———

He mutters, " They are gone, alas !
Into the valley, up the Pass,
To happy homes they love so well,
In dreamy vale and sheltered dell ;
And joy is theirs, and cherisht lore,
But I am alien evermore."

———

Then, raising his voice till it sweetly rang
From mountain to valley, the minstrel sang.

———

AWEN'S SONG.

" Farewell to the land of the bards and the sages !
    Vain all disputing and vain all delay ;
Time will be merciful, yet on his pages
    Constantly writeth he, ' Passing away.'

———

" To customs antique, and to memories hoary,
    Long your hoar elders in fondness may cling ;
But new generations will weave the land's story,
    In forms that to her new glory will bring.

———

" Perchance it were better and nobler and wiser
   Loving to cling to you lifelong and leal ;
But in the high court of the mind an adviser
   Other and stronger is pleading, I feel.

———

" Heart's blood and arm's strength to you freely I'd render,
   Land of my fathers, if danger o'erfrowned,
Yet patriot true and true country's defender
   Is he who makes his loved country renowned.

———

" Renowned not alone in arms' terrors and glories—
   War is degrading to man, and his bane—
But weaving the wisest and worthiest of stories,
   Lightening sorrow and lessening pain.

———

" Proud sons of the mountains, you sing in each fastness,
   ' Land of our fathers, dear ever shalt be ; '
Nor dream that the earth in its uttermost vastness
   Alone is the home of the great and the free.

———

" Nor remember that but a small part of the Island
   Is left you and yours to boast of and prize ;
Your fathers were lords over lowland and highland,
   Knowing no bounds but the seas and the skies.

———

" Widen man's sympathies, God of creation !
  Stifle his selfishness, quicken his love ;
Let him know the whole land as only one nation,
  As 'tis known to Thine eye all-seeing above."

The voice went echoing up the hill,
  And sounding down the valley far,
And ofttimes still those tones will thrill
  The glens where fairy dwellers are.

And Awen went his lonely way,
Yet where he went there's none can say;
But the Aneurin's dreamful eye
Sees the unseen in earth and sky,
And he anon will further tell
What next the wandering Childe befell.

H

CANTO FOURTH.

CANTO FOURTH.

HE that hath wandered the whole weary day
  In some lone country whither he before
  Had never gone, and may go never more,
Feels how forlorn the traveller on his way
Drags his late footsteps prayerful, prone to stay,
  Yet fearful stops not, doubting struggles on
  Till the last glimpse of life and hope be gone,
Then helpless sinks, all thought of succour o'er,
On some dread headland's edge or dark deep water's shore.

  Oh, stay, bright day, with the glad and gay,
    Leave not the joyous-hearted ;
  Linger long with the children at play,
    Nor let dear friends be parted.
  Night, you may come to the weary and old,
    Bringing rest to the many who moan,
  But wrap not now in your ebony coils
  Him who along yon cloud-height toils,
    All weary and lorn and lone.

Oh, let him not wander unaware
To dread ravine or forest drear,
Nor yet to fenceless tarn or pathless wold.

———

List to the tinkling of the rills
Down-skipping from the rocky hills,
   Hark to the river's roar ;
Oh, hear the ocean's solemn roll,
It sways and sweeps from pole to pole,
   And thunders on the shore !
Mysterious sounds float on the breeze,
Mysterious forms the dreamer sees,
Mysterious thoughts crowd in the mind,
Far from the haunts of human kind.

———

All things seem changed above and below,
   And the world is hushed with dread ;
Gone from the west is the sunset glow,
   And the last grey gleam is fled.
The glory of day is faded and past,
The gloom of night o'er the earth is cast,
And the wan white moon through dusky space
Glides with a grave and ghostly grace.
Queen of the black night realm is she,
Supremely pale in her purity.
Grandly beautiful, fair and free,
Her white feet skim the silvern sea,

And dance over lakes and rivers and rills,
In deepest valleys, on highest hills.
Oh, softer the light of her face so fair
And sweeter its lure than the sun's glare,
And it moves the hectorly heart of man
To holier moods than Phœbus can!

'Tis dreadful night, yet beautiful !
And over the land a soothing lull
Drops down like balm, and silence steals
Over half the world, and man now feels
A calm by day he cannot know.
Harsh sounds are husht, and soft and low
The murmurs of the night go by.
Earth communes with the star-gemmed sky,
And with abated breath she hears
The music of far passing spheres.
The sighing night wind whispers, " Rest ; "
And sobs and moanings long suppressed
Float upward, mingling as they rise
In one grand' prayer for Paradise.

Still over the palled and muffled scene
The moon moves up the sky serene.
Oh, welcome light, sweet Queen of Night,
On pathless plain and dizzy height !

And praised be He who set on high
Such silent glory in the sky !

———

Lo, yonder wayward youth !   What dread
Illusion or despair hath led
Him to the verge of that grey cliff ?
His supple form all cold and stiff
In Death's embrace, might soon have been
In tangled depths of the ravine,
Did not her silvern radiance show
The dark and dire abyss below !
Stop, Awen Weahl ! no farther stray ;
A hundred deaths now bar thy way !
They'll vanish when the day returns.
The poorest wanderer some rest earns.

———

Repose you there—those crumbled walls
Of old encompassed princely halls,
Within which many a festive scene,
And many a foul debauch hath been.
There often, when the feud was o'er,
Armed men caroused and raved and swore,
While bearded bards sang of their might,
And glorious deeds achieved in fight,
And bright-eyed dames with awe and fear
Their sanguinary tales would hear.

———

Perhaps where thou dost lay thy head
  A prince lay ne'er to rise again;
A princess may have lain there dead,
  By jealous spouse in slumber slain;
A warrior true and brave, perchance,
Fell there by thrust of traitor's lance;
A tyrant there mayhap did feel
The vengeance of a wronged man's steel.
But fear you not; whate'er has been
Can be no more. Rest you serene,
With wandering spent.

           He is at rest!
Pass gently, breezes, o'er his breast;
Bend softly, Cynthia, o'er his face,
Illumined with your own pale grace;
Roll softlier, sea; and you, bright streams,
Blend not too loudly with his dreams
Your endless songs.

         And now he deems
The summer sun his lengthened way
Pursues with unobstructed ray,
And he himself has reached the while
The precincts of a spacious pile,
A crumbling castle grim and old,
Yet still defiant, massive, bold.

Long 'twas the home of warlike kings,
Though now the suppliant ivy clings
About the disembattled walls,
And in its ivied towers and halls
The dismal owls their vigils keep,
And vagrant beasts securely sleep.

With cautious, slow, and reverent pace
Moves Awen through the hallowed place,
Till in his mind strange fancies spring,
And ghostly sounds around him ring—
Of scenes of treachery and of strife;
Of wrong for wrong, and life for life;
Of murders done in maddened mood,
Or wrought through years in coldest blood;
Of torture, tyranny, and treason,
That strain his eyes and rack his reason.

Each dark recess appears to teem
　With grizzly forms with blazing eyes;
The slightest sound becomes a scream,
　Each weird wind's wail some victim's cries;
And when to the dank keep he crept,
　Where kings had groaned their lives away,
Where queens for mercy vainly wept,
　And maidens' locks with grief turned grey,

Then changed the scene.   The castle rose
  In all its pristine pride and state ;
Again the silent sentry goes
  With steady tramp by bridge and gate.
The watchful warrior in his tower
  Looks out athwart the land afar,
And contemplates his martial power
  To turn the tide of feudal war.

———

It is a place of charm and life,
A place where might and beauty reign,
Prepared alike for peace or strife,
For clang of war or festive strain.

———

The scene was grand to Awen's view ;
It filled his heart with joy and pride,
And as his admiration grew,
  In blissful ecstasy he cried,
"How beautiful, how brave !"   And then
He saw he was not there alone—
At hand a throng of courtly men,
Whose converse had an ancient tone.
"A Kelt !" said one, with hostile show ;
"A Waal," they cried, "o'errun his tether !"
And then with stately step and slow
They moved towards the Childe together.

———

" A Waal !" they said ; " defiant too !
To Offa's well without ado ;
In the Hadean depths below
He'll find surcease for earthly woe."

———

Then Awen Wealh : " Let one but dare,
And by my ancestry I swear—
Whose noble memory I cherish—
Not I alone, sirs, there will perish !"

———

Derisive laughter answered him,
And said the foremost, tall and trim,
" Thou wouldst defiance hurl at me ?
Thou swearest by thy ancestry ?
Od's blood !   It is a merry jest.
Thou darest and thou swearest !   Best
Thou prayedst."

———

"Nay, not I should pray
To such as thou, or such as they.
Be what you seem, and you will give
Me chance to win the right to live,
Then if I fail, so, let me die ;
I fall as fell my ancestry,
Face to the foe.   Come one, or all ;
I yield not, whether I stand or fall."

———

Prompt to the front the gallants sprang,
The place with shouts and laughter rang,
And seemed it that in very scorn
Awen at once had been downborne.
But cried the leader, " Stay your hands !
He dies who dares cross my commands !
'Faith, 'tis the veriest braggart youth.
He swears by his forefathers, sooth !
Next will the kitchen scullions swear
By those who did them basely bear.
He is unarmed, too.   Zounds ! a brand.
Give him a weapon to his hand,
Then let some hair-brained, beardless page
In merest frolic him engage."

" Take back the sneer, sir, in your teeth !
The best among you shall unsheath.
Even as you see, unarmed I stand
Obedient to the law's command,
For, know, men long have ceased to need
Or lance or sword to make hearts bleed ;
Yet though my body be not charmed,
Do thou thy worst I'm still unharmed.
So give me hilt of sword to clasp,
And you shall find my weakling grasp

Not unaccustomed is to wield
Such weapon's weight. My faith my shield."

———

"'Tis bravely said, yet said, in truth,
As empty boast by wanton youth.
Still, thy demeanour likes me well.
Who art thou, and whence comest—tell?"

———

"I come from Dynver Towers, and know
The life-floods through my veins that flow,
Have started from such ancient springs
As well might match with any king's.
My sire a knight as fair and sound
As ever graced the Table Round.
Then should I fight in my degree,
None meaner I'll engage than thee,
Though Offa's self he be I dare
To mortal combat free and fair."

———

"Be it so, proud boy. Or wrong or right,
Sirs, he with none but me shall fight;
'Tis mine alone to pluck the flower
Of knighthood's hope from Dynver Tower."

———

A sword to Awen soon they wheel;
Like lightning flashed the circling steel,

Covering as with a shield of flame
His elsewise unprotected frame.
He caught it deftly by the blade
  And held it upward like a cross.
He bowed his head and silent prayed,
   Then grasped the hilt through twirl and toss.

———

The opponents pose, the weapons clash,
From point to heel they hiss and flash,
And fast and fierce the combat grows.
Mailed knights were never worthier foes ;
In point and guard well matched the twain.
But Awen soon must strive in vain
  His foe's maturer strength against ;
Yet, cool of head and firm of nerve,
From fiercest cut he will not swerve,
  And every lunge is bravely fenced.

———

But foul mishap more dire may be.
Than strength and skill of foe, we see.
Lo ! wild and wide his weapon cleaves
The air, and all unguarded leaves
His brow and breast. Oh, wherefore is't
His erst firm footing he hath missed ?
A hidden trailing ivy root
Hath in its toils his nimble foot,

And Awen falls ! His foeman's blade
Comes circling downward on his head
With fatal force ! Nay, 'twill not be !
Though shirt of mail nor helm hath he,
The other's brand comes harmless down
On Awen, on his right knee thrown,
And bends across his forehead fair
   As supple as a wand of willow,
And makes no more impression there
   Than a head on a granite pillow !

What charm, what power, what mystic spell,
Wrought his escape so strange to tell?
Behold, 'tis she ! Oh, sweet command !
More potent is her wee white hand
Than greatest Herculean might
That ever despoiled a warrior wight.
" A truce !" she says ; "your conflict cease !
Man's noblest attribute is peace."

Not one then stirred, but, filled with awe,
Nor realizing what they saw,
They stood abashed with eyes down-turned
To hide the fire that in them burned.

Joy's very form, Love's very queen,
And Beauty's very self ! Serene

As spring day's dawn on orient heights
Straight from the sun's gold gates alights,
Dispensing Day's supernal glow
Along the awakening lands below,
So on yon disembattled wall,
  Moss-covered, ivy-clad, and high,
Now stands that maiden fair and tall
  Against the vaulted, violet sky;
And her white arm uplifted gleams
  And flashes in the lucent air,
As through an oriel window streams
  The softened sunshine on her hair.
From her white brow enwreathed with flowers
  Down to her arched feet small and white,
She shines between the mouldering towers,
  A figure of celestial light.

———

Sweet form, of perfect symmetry!
It is a vision fair to see,
  Evolved from formless space.
What heart to your charms could be cold,
What eye in anger could behold
  Your pure, seraphic grace?
More white than snow your forehead seems;
Your smile with roseate radiance beams;

I

Your cheeks rose-tinted are ;
Your lips red rose-blooms wet with dew ;
Your eyes profound of violet hue,
   Each brilliant as a star.

———

Forget-me-nots and lilies deck
Her lovely head and ivory neck ;
And all around her form is thrown
Her rippling hair of amber-brown,
And through its countless silken threads
The sun his golden lustre sheds,
So that her loveliness is bound
With glinting glories all around.
From under her flowing drapery,
White, filmy, folding, and vapoury,
Like phosphorescent gleams and fleet
Peep now and then her twinkling feet,
And all her movements seem to be
Parts of some graceful harmony.

———

She looked, nay, not in wrath, but more
Compassion those fair features wore ;
She spoke, and every accent fell
Like music indescribable,
To sway the heart or soothe the sense
To rapture or to impotence

As chanced her will to be, and as
Her purpose or her pleasure was.

———

With charming cadence hear her say,
" Oh, wherefore such unseemly fray?
Still brave and free all hearts must be
 That beat in Britain great and pure,
In harmony with the great sea
 That guards and keeps the land secure.
For ever hence all men must feel
In this Wiht Isle no tyrant's heel
 Must ever rest, or any foe
To Britain's race or Britain's weal.
 One people hand in hand we go,
Still heart to heart, and soul to soul,
Race blent with race, a mighty whole,
To form an empire that shall be
The grandest in Earth's history,
Where no race shall itself esteem
To be o'er all the rest supreme."

———

As shadows flee before the dawn,
Those forms mysterious had withdrawn;
But Awen could not go, nor raise
His eyes to meet her chastening gaze.
Then on his ears the softened swell
Of that rare voice more sweetly fell,

As thus she sang, nor high, nor low,
But with a thrilling, fervent flow :

THE MAIDEN'S SONG.

The far-flowing streamlet
   To ocean meanders ;
The child in his dreamlet
   To brighter lands wanders
Than that of the mountains
   And music-filled valleys
With streams and with fountains
   Where Liberty rallies.

———

Is Awen Wealh yearning
   For gain or adventure ?
Or is his soul spurning
   Control or rude censure ?
Or is his heart dreading
   The tempest that gathers,
In fury o'erspreading
   The land of his fathers?

———

Rash Childe ! in his dreaming
   Of lands that are fairer,
And scenes that are gleaming
   With loveliness rarer ;

And in his long roaming
  In hope or in sorrow,
His thoughts will be homing
  To-morrow, to-morrow.

———

Intense is the lightning
  That flashes from glances
Of dusky eyes bright'ning
  With maidenly fancies ;
Delightful the laughter
  Of Cambria's dark daughters,
Like sounds that come after
  The rippling of waters.

———

Entrancing their voices
  Through Cambria ringing ;
The nation rejoices
  In songs they are singing.
Her sons have bold spirits,
  Their deeds are recorded,
And Awen inherits
  What fame hath awarded.

———

In the ocean the streamlet
  Will vanish for ever ;
Dispelled be the dreamlet
  By Life's long endeavour ;

In cities' dense throngings
In broadways and alleys,
Will come intense longings
For mountains and valleys.

———

While sang the maiden Awen stood
Spell-bound, yet swayed by varying mood,
Now urged to interpose, and then
Abashed, subdued, and mute again ;
Now boldly shoots an upward glance,
And moves his foot as to advance,
Then halts, and with his eyes depressed
Lays hand upon his burning breast ;
Now o'er his brow a crimson flush
Would quickly spread, then with a rush
Back to his heart the life-tide rolled.
By turns elated, heated, cold,
He heard the sweet, rebukeful strain,
And meekly followed the refrain.
When she had sung, he turned his eyes
To where past Vaga's stream uprise
The Walian Hills to heaven allied,
And with soft, quivering voice replied.

AWEN'S REPLY.

There may be lands fairer 'neath sunnier skies,
Where balmier breezes through orange groves blow,

But I love the land where yon airy peaks rise,
    Where fast-falling waters thro' hazel glens flow.

I seek not adventure, nor sigh for romance ;
    I care not an aimless rover to be ;
I heed not the world or its frivolous dance,
    But yearn for the land that in freedom is free.

Where is that spot where the minstrel may never
    Tremble the name of his country to tell?
Where is that place where no people has ever
    Claimed on its soil the sole freedom to dwell?

'Tis not in the land long sacred and cherished ;
    Not on the plains that our forefathers trod ;
Not on the soil that received them who perished,
    Devoted to liberty, country, and God !

    I know not if his song was done,
    But he could sing no more.   As one
    Deep moved she stood, her eyes
    Far fixed, communing with the skies,
    Rapt for a moment; then she sighed,
       "Childe, 'tis a sweet yet bitter song !"
    "As bitter as my heart," he cried,
       "And spirit made sensitive to wrong."

"Made sensitive to wrong?" she mused,
With slow-moved lips and looks diffused,
Like one repeating in a dream;
Then sudden with new light would gleam
Her eyes and flash, and quick, as though
Some distant sound to catch, tiptoe
  She stood, while instantly her hand
Flew upward pearl-like and glistening
To her wee white ear, there listening,
  A marvel of sweet form and grand,
To sounds that fall not on this sphere
That mortal ears may ever hear.
But soon with earthward inclination
She gave him sweet interpretation :

———

"Let the minstrel's heart rejoice ;
  Time shall end his cause for plaint.
Thus," she said, "I heard a voice,
  Hear again distinct though faint.
Time is working change on change,
And the civilizing range,
Ever widening, will extend
Through the ages without end,
Till all pagan ways have passed
Out of mode and mind at last,
And the mightiest people be
Those who wander far and free,

Over land and over water
Without greed and without slaughter,
Carrying freedom, light, and right
Where have been dread wrong and might,
Liberty to every land
As they love it who command.

———

" Race distinctions will be past,
  And the age of clanship gone ;
To fraternities more vast
  Men will steadily move on.
Time will be when by their deeds
  Men and women shall be judged,
Not by race and not by creeds,
  Rights enjoyed nor rights begrudged ;
Each by individual worth,
None by borrowed fame nor birth.
And the nations as they swell,
  And the empires as they spread,
Will in pride of memory tell
  Of the lustre they have shed
O'er their growth and generation,
World-surrounding federation !

———

" Old the scheme is as the sun,
  With whose lighting 'twas begun ;

With his dark'ning it will cease,
Followed by eternal peace.

———

" Full the past of sorrow and pain ;
Gone its struggles noble or vain ;
Evil were the man's desires
Who would stir its smouldering fires.

———

" Let the ministrel not bewail
Perished ages, but forehail
Cycles unevolved from time
With their unwrought works sublime ;
For the far unfolding light
　Of the future will reveal,
Foremost in the failing fight
　Of the false against the real,
Those by truest instincts led—
　Noblest principles constrained,
Till the false be down and dead,
　And the true fore'er maintained.

———

" Britain's sons are ever those,
　And her pride must ever be,
Who her history compose,
　Working out her destiny.
Those are truest who go forth
East and west and south and north,

And no seas, or depths, or heights
Shall proscribe their acts or rights.
Britain is a mighty land,
  But a mightier yet shall be,
And her worthiest sons shall stand
  First of her nobility—
Foremost in the glorious, grand,
  Broadening nationality.

———

" Antique forms they must amend
  Who'd be Britain's pioneers,
Higher forms to comprehend
  In the upward rolling years.
Action is the health of nations,
  Wider, weightier, worthier still,
And succeeding generations
  Work with ever vaster will;
Wisdom forth with Progress sallies,
Folly with Tradition dallies."

———

Then round her rose-red lips there wreathed
A beauteous smile, and briefly breathed
She restfully, while pearl-like white
Her small teeth gleamed between the slight
Lips lightly parted. Next was broken
Silence with this directly spoken :

———

" Is the new light on you stealing,
Glories of new times revealing?
Blank the page is of to-morrow,
Yesterday's is blurred with sorrow!
Will you in repining mood
On the latter vainly brood,
Or the former contemplate
With new hope and faith elate?
Is the waning of the day
  Ever lovelier than the dawn?
Is not that advancing ray
  Brighter than the light withdrawn?"

———

" Bright and beautiful being!
With vision far-seeing
Down the depths of my soul,
  Through Futurity's veil;
Time brings many changes,
Arranges, deranges,
But man cannot in his whole
  Native character fail."

———

" Hark! I hear that voice once more,
Stronger, clearer than before:
Great the people's aspirations
In great blending, broadening nations.

In the hearts of heroes rise
Yearnings for some great emprise,
And their glorious works and worth
Raise the nations of their birth ;
But a braggart people's boast
Noblest nations censure most,
For no honour, glory, or fame
Comes of praising one's own name.

———

" Love of country in some breasts
Only selfishness attests :
Broadening principles must sway
   All the world's community ;
Manlier motives must have play,
   Making grander history.

———

" Britons spreading o'er the earth-face,
   Dominant on land and sea,
Claim a planet for their birthplace,
   World-wide nationality ;
And the nations as they rise,
   And the peoples as they spread,
Know no spot beneath the skies
   Where they may not proudly tread."

———

"Such were the thoughts," then Awen mused,
" That loomed upon my mind confused ;

But now they rise distinct and whole,
And lighten like a sun my soul."

———

Then she, " How tardily men solve
Life's ordinations, and evolve
Man's certain attribute, to rise
Above race prejudice, and wise
Perceive that One divine who wrought
Supreme the universe from naught,
Made no land fair with special grace
To bless above all else one race ! "

———

" I would rejoice if men could say,
'One God alone we know and pray ;
The world is His, and everywhere
One land shall be our love and care.'
But, ah ! such narrowness of mind
Still marks the doings of mankind,
That sympathy and heart and soul
Few acts of man towards man control,
While ignorance and prejudice
Find vent in many a wrong and vice.
Even here," he said, " in this fair Isle,
Men will employ all wit and wile
In limiting the liberties
Of others, who in naught displease

Save that they prize an ancient name
And title in this land of fame—
Would strip them of long-cherished rights,
Old privilege, and sacred rites;
Would mock and taunt them, even wrest
From them all things endeared and blest;
Their ancient customs would destroy,
And in their degradation joy."

"The character is too severe,"
The maid said softly; "yet I fear
It hath some truth in't.   Great the need
Of magnanimity indeed
'Twixt man and man, and state and state.
Love's throne is oft usurpt by Hate,
And Might is King of Right, and his
Domain, too vast, extending is.
There men will swagger who the fight
Have won, and, thinking wrong to right,
Right deeply wrong.   Oft hardly used
The stranger is, but more abused
The manner than the man; still quick
The braggart, clownish, choleric
Are made the butt of jest and jeer,
No matter whence they come, or near

Or far—from hills where Chaos reigns,
Green flowery vales, or sunny plains."

———

She paused, but archly added then,
" Unreasoning oft the ways of men,
But they are not all good and grand
Or blameless even in Cambrian Land."

———

"They have their failings," quick he said ;
"Their faults are many, some are dread.
But let it pass, and by the spell
You've bound me with I pray you tell—"

———

Awen stopped short.   He'd raised his eyes
In treaty for her name.   To his surprise,
That form so beautiful was gone,
And the bright light that round her shone.
No one was near !   He thought it strange,
And he was conscious of a change
Come over him.   He felt as they
Who love and lose all in a day.

———

On those grim walls the sun had ceased to glow,
Where sunshine was there is but shadow now;
And like that pile his soul to him must seem,
Reft of its glory and the sunset gleam,
And there he lingers, in double gloom the while
All darkly rapt as darkness wraps the pile.

K

CANTO FIFTH.

CANTO FIFTH.

THERE is a sight that is not of the sense
    Corporeal; from the material sun
It cannot draw its wondrous competence :
    'Tis with the vision of the angels one.
There is a power of hand and heart immense,
    That doth not to the earthly frame belong,
    And he that hath that sight and power is strong,
And blest beyond man's best intelligence,
For his are glorious dreams and God's eternal song.

Oh, would that I this while might feel
    The glow and consummating fire,
The passion, prescience, and the zeal
    That thrilled the immortal master's lyre !
Then should my song the echo be
Of those sweet strains eternally
That in that land so sweetly swell
Where ancient bards and minstrels dwell.

And all the scenes of glory great
They wander through in changeless state
I'd picture for the world's delight.
The sweetest sounds, the grandest sight,
That ever yet were heard or seen
By ears of mortal man or een.
But that the gods forbid, and I
Can but invoke my muse to try
In strains I may command to tell
What later to the Childe befel.

———

Long time he wondered, doubted, feared
How that sweet form had disappeared.
Mysteriously as any fay
She came and passed again away;
And whence she came, and where she went,
He pondered in astonishment;
Yet no solution to him came,
But fiercer burned that kindling flame.

———

He would have shouted high and low,
  What though he roused the echoes all,
But, what dismay! he did not know
  By what sweet name the maid to call.
Still, he must call. Though meaningless,
He must find vent for his distress;

And so he called, in whispers first,
And all the welkin seemed to burst
With wondrous whispers ! But again
He called aloud with might and main.
He called a shade, a nameless sprite,
Still louder, through the silent night,
Till universal space seemed filled
With his sole voice, all else was stilled !

He was o'erwhelmed. He could not bear
His voice alone to hear in th' air,
And yet from heights and depths profound
There came to him no other sound.
Then he could call no more ; 'twas vain,
For only Echo called again,
And she was everywhere, mad sprite !
In lowest depth and highest height.

Irresolute he stood. 'Twas plain
To quit the scene he strove in vain.
" It could not be a dream," he said,
  " Albeit she seemed for earth too fair;
If not, she cannot far have fled,
  Or vanished into formless air.

Oh, beauteous maiden !" then he cried,
" Where flee you or where do you hide ? "

———

Again with peering eyes he passed
From the first chamber to the last,
With beating heart and 'bated breath,
But found nor maiden fair nor wraith.
" Could so much loveliness," he thought,
" Be merest fancy, nowhere, naught ? "

———

Again those grounds that once were fair,
   Though long disordered, round the pile,
He swept in hope to find her there
   And catch again her radiant smile ;
Then on the towers and turrets stood
   To scan the country far and wide,
But whatsoe'er the scene he viewed,
   No maiden there could flee or hide.
In vain he further fared and strode
Down mazy lane and winding road
Which from the castle led away
To scenes more modern and more gay.
And peer and pry wherever he might,
   Through copse and brake, and o'er the wold,
No human figure met his sight,
   No eye of blue or tress of gold ;

No maid again or sprite he sees,
Nor any voice hears on the breeze.

———

It was too clear the form he sought
Had vanished like a passing thought,
  Or like a snowflake in a stream,
Or like delusive Hope's transition,
Or like a wild and frenzied vision
  Before awakening reason's beam.

———

Ah! there are dreams of many kinds,
More varied than men's moods and minds,
And what are dreams, what fancies merely,
  What acts done in the waking glow,
What hard material facts, full clearly
  No mortal man can always know.

———

It is not strange, though strange it seems,
That even in dreams we've other dreams,
And oft we think in slumbers deep
A wary, wakeful watch we keep
On friend's fair faith or foe's intrigue,
And to sweet sleep ourselves betake,
And dream we from a dream awake.

———

In sleep the waking life, revived
In the quick brain, again is lived,

And in our waking acts we seem
But to retrace some vanished dream.

———

So whether we wake or whether we sleep
   Is questionable ever,
But much we laugh and much we weep
   As flows an endless river,
Because our spirits swell and sweep
   With strong constrained endeavour,
And why their sinuous course they keep
   One may, perhaps, know never,
    Not even the longest liver.
Impressions of our acts remain
Indelible upon the brain,
And things indefinite seem real,
While forms material grow ideal.

———

When from our baseless dreams we wake,
Our wills and acts some fashion take
And force from what the forms have been
That in our visions we have seen,
And joy or grief, and love or hate,
Our waking minds will stimulate,
As wild or calm, as foul or fair,
The sleeping moods and fancies were.

———

And well men may, when wrapt in sleep,
Of time a different record keep,
And count a weary night and day
In one brief moment passed away.
Now, Awen Wealh, in fancy free,
Had deemed that long and searchingly
He scanned and scoured the country round,
But never more that fair form found ;
Then, in despair and weary grown,
On the green sward he laid him down,
And rested still on yonder hill
Where shines the white moon wan and still.

What is the feeling new and strange
That in his soul hath wrought such change?
Why should he linger on the spot ?
An hour ago he knew it not.
What makes it now so hard to go
That grimly, crumbling castle fro' ?
Ah ! wot you not love's fire is lit ?
And wot you not who kindled it ?
"She is as wise as fair," he sighed ;
" Her like may not on earth abide."

Lo, is it morning's glory now
Enwreaths Craig Eirey's lofty brow

Or is it Aurora's fitful light
That crowns the monarch mountain's height?

———

No mundane sheen is that, I ween,
Now by the Childe of Dynver seen.
Night's deepest hour is hardly flown,
And Awen's wondering eye is shown
No earthly form that from afar
Comes with the radiance of a star;
No mortal voices these he hears,
Like music from more blissful spheres.

First Voice.

Arise, O Childe, from earthly song,
To join th' immortal minstrel throng;
   Morwyn commands!
We come to make the spirit free
To soar and sing eternally
   In brighter lands.
     Arise, Arise!

Second Voice.

Come, emancipated spirit,
To the realms the bards inherit;
   Follow, follow! thence we lead,

And thou shalt behold the glory
Of the great of earthly story,
  Minstrels' missions are decreed.
    Come, come !

Voices in the Distance.

Exult and rejoice with heart and with voice,
  For Morwyn's minstrel Childe
Is coming along in a glory of song
  From Cambria beguiled.
    Awen Wealh, hail !

Chorus of Voices.

Hail, Awen Wealh, hail !
Morwyn, mother of all light,
Calls thee to her regions bright,
Where the bardic sons of old
You shall hear and eke behold—
See their bay-bound brows and grand ;
Hear their songs and understand ;
Join their wanderings far and free
Over land and lake and sea,
Thorough scenes of beauty rare,
Ever changing, ever fair
In a brilliant breezy air,
Free from shadow, free from glare ;

Full of grand harmonious sounds
To the region's utmost bounds ;
Full of loveliness and light,
. Everything that charms the sight ;
Full of perfumes that invite
Every sense to keen delight ;
Full of joy without alloy,
Pleasures that will never cloy ;
Whither anguish, care, and pain
Never wring the poet's brain.
Poet spirit, Morwyn calls
Thee to her eternal halls.
   Awen Wealh, hail,
    Hail, all hail !

He reaches now the mystic shore
Where, as men learn in bardic lore,
 The spirits of poets dwell ;
Where Morwyn, goddess of the sea,
And goddess, too, of poesie,
Gives them glory eternally,
 And youth immutable.
And all the mysteries of that world
Before his wondering eyes unfurled
 Are marvellous to tell.

Above him spreads a heaven of blue,
  More blue than known to mortal een ;
Around him meadows bright and new,
  And greener than on earth are seen,
Ev'n where those charmèd circles grew,
  And nocturn revels of fays have been.

———

Forests varied and vast he sees
Of delicate plants and spreading trees,
And through the shimmer and shadeless shine
Of sprays that quiver and intertwine,
Of boughs that dangle and interlace,
Of foliage touched with a wonderful grace
Of form, and tint, and tone, and glaze ;
Through which the glory as of the blaze
Of myriads of blooms whose lights combined
Might even the sight of a seraph blind.

———

He sees quaint fountains, silvern streams,
Sparkle and flash in the varying gleams
  Of a luminous atmosphere ;
Breathes perfumed breezes soft and sweet ;
And mellow mingling melodies greet
  His rapt and ravished ear.
Scans many a lake's pellucid breast
Lying along in its dreamy rest,

By softest zephyrs fanned,
And never the marvellous mirror's stirred
More than the sky by the wings of a bird,
    Or mere by an angler's hand.

In gleaming robes of pleasing hues,
Moving among the scenes they choose,
Brighter than fancy paints or dreams,
Joying in many delightful themes,
Awen marvelling gazes on
The great whose names in song have shone,
Such music hears as mortal bard
Never in earthly form hath heard.
Yet all these thrilling sounds above,
In tones of joy and peace and love,
He hears one voice that instantly
Fills him with deep anxiety.

'Tis like a voice he has heard before.
Ah, is it that sweet voice once more?
Not that, but yet of charming sweetness.
It is the fulness and completeness
Of rarest tones that until now
Unfrequently and faint would flow
Down by the current of his soul.
It is the gathered sacred whole

Of scattered, fragmentary tones
That hovered long above the zones
Of his thought-world, but ne'er would pierce
The heart of his heart's universe.

———

Whose is the voice? 'Twill quickly be
Revealed, impatient Childe, to thee.
Whose is that form? 'Tis not that one
You late have yearned to look upon,
Yet is it beautiful beyond
What brain too swift and heart too fond
Can conjure up in hues all bright
To fascinate the mystic sight.
But let thy anxious soul rejoice;
Behold the form, and hark the voice!
He sees, he hears; no more I may
To human eyes and ears convey.

———

It is a beauteous form, in truth,
That glides towards the admiring youth,
Arrayed in flowing robes of blue,
Alight with gems of brightest hue,
And crystal, like the pearly dowers
That beautify the loveliest flowers,
And round her waist a zone more bright
Than is the Milky Way at night.

———

Her eyes are dusky-dark and bright,
And flashing with enchanting light,
Illumining her lovely presence
As with celestial iridescence ;
Her locks are blacker than the wing
Of rarest raven, and they fling
Their long luxuriance and sleek
Adown her arched white brows and cheek
Tinged with a pink-rose radiance,
Then sweep in free exuberance
Round her white throat and snow-pure bosom.
And many a rich-hued bloom and blossom,
With green and glossy leaflets bound,
Wreathe her small queenly head around.
On each white dimpled arm behold
Resplendent bracelets, hoops of gold ;
And in her tapering rose-tipt hand
She waves an amber-lucent wand.

———

Now could you mark her dark eyes' flashes
Beneath arched brows and silken lashes,
How they illume the forehead white
As lightnings play along the height
Of tall white cliffs, and on white waves
Leap far below into dark caves.
As she approached the astonished Childe,
No maiden ever so sweetly smiled,

And never could heart of bard rejoice
At sweeter music than her voice.

———

"We greet you joyfully as ours,
Childe Awen Wealh from Dynver Tow'rs,
For who loves Morwyn well," said she,
"Must be forefraught with love for thee,
And who to me are faithful, true,
Shall true and faithful be to you.
Know I am Credwen, she whose part
Hath been to inspire the minstrel's heart,
And over Cambrian hills and vales
While time endures. my power prevails.
I taught you first the art divine
To weave sweet song and count it mine,
And lo, this garland I have now
Here woven for your ample brow."

———

Then Credwen from her girdle drew
    A chaplet of the choicest flowers,
The fairest in that land that grew,
    And fairer far than bloom in ours.

———

How sweet the melody, how bright !
Rapt Awen listened with delight
To her sweet voice, and watched the while
Her dark eyes beam, her witching smile ;

But when she paused, he tried in vain
To make her answer fair again.
With shame his awkwardness he felt,
And mutely at her feet then knelt
And forward bent his head ; but she
Smiled only more enchantingly,
　　Half singing and half saying,
　　The wreath on his head laying,
"Hail, Awen Wealh, the light to be
Of Britain's future minstrelsie ! "

Then Awen rose, with kindling eye,
Meek but not mute, to make reply.
"Oh, fair Credwen ! " he thus essayed,
"Genius of Poesie, who swayed
The hearts and harps of bards whose lays
Were Britain's pride in olden days,
Whose tones were heard through the Wiht Isle
To make War frown or Pleasure smile.
Sweet guide of all the great and good,
Of all the immortal brotherhood !
Great joy hath sometimes thrilled my soul,
And yearnings swelling past control
With lyre and lay to emulate
That antique bardic band and great ;
And I have longed to make my tongue
Heard pleadingly the gods among,

When I have seen the sweet young flowers
Long pining for the genial showers,
And thought I heard their piteous cry
As on earth's breast they drooped to die;
When I have heard Earth's children crying,
   And seen them dead,
And no one heeded, though while dying
   They cried for bread.

———

" But, ah ! the song that once prevailed
In Britain is no longer hailed
With joy or grace.   The gods, 'tis said,
Regard both song and language dead,
Yet great my joy, Credwen, to greet
You thus, and share your smiles so sweet,
Though well I know unmerited
By aught that I have done or said.
Too weak, alas ! my song to move
Men's hearts to wrath or gentle love,
Or stir their souls to passions high,
To bravely dare or nobly die ;
But to your will should I demur,
So faint to do, so prone to err ?
Nay, Maiden of the Sacred Hill,
Command your minstrel to your will."

———

" The bardic fire in you is pent,
And it shall find in song full vent ;
But learn," she said, " till racked and riven
With longing fierce, it is not given
To soul of bard or sage to know
Surcease or source of mundane woe.
Woe comes not here.   Now pass with me
Through marvel, maze, and mystery.

———

" 'Twas I," she added, "from your birth
Watched all your moods from grief to mirth.
I led you from the childish rout
Of headlong chase and wrestling bout,
And proudly watched you, fancy-wrought,
Immersed in more than childish thought,
Lifting your wide and wondering eyes
In searching glance to clouds and skies.
I urged your boyish feet to stray
To lonely foss and ruin grey,
Through forests hoar and woodlands green,
Through fairy glen and wild ravine ;
Day after day by purling streams
I stored your brain with beauteous dreams,
And filled your eyes with scenes more rare
Than found in painters' pictures are ;
Up trackless hills to lofty heights,
I watched your solitary flights,

And taught your heart such pleasures were
More joyous than the worldly share.

" With joy I saw yon minstrel true
The mouthing multitude eschew
That overrun the Cambrian Land,
Self-called, alas ! her bardic band ;
But they shall pass, and purer song
Will roll the Cymric hills along.
Now let us hie where Morwyn waits,
Lo ! where they ope the crystal gates."

So Awen on with Credwen passed
In a sweet spell, and hand-in-hand,
Through meads of asphodel and grassed
As green and soft as fairyland,
Till burst upon his dazzled sight
The glories of a scene too bright
For mortal eyes, and mortal hand
Could not the immortal power command
To picture to the mortal sense
Its grandeur and magnificence.

Grand gleams a palace carved in light,
Vast, yet transparent, wondrous white,
Yet prism-like refracting beams
Of every sun and star that streams

Light into space.   There tower and shine
Countless carved columns crystalline,
And loftier than the tallest pine.
The floors far-spreading, strangely wrought,
Seem the long motion to have caught
Of the vast sea, and every tinge,
Grey, green, and blue, and foamy fringe.

———

From chased and spangled capitals on high
    Spring sweeping arcs of wide and graceful span,
Beneath a varied, panelled canopy
    All pencilled on the rarest, richest plan ;
The walls, all massive yet all clear and bright,
    Are carved and caverned in a curious way—
All forms are there that give the eye delight,
    And revelling fancy universal play.
All ways it fronts, the marvellous edifice,
    And every front some sculptured glory shows—
Poems and histories wrought in hills of ice,
    And flowers of fancy in perennial snows.
Tall spires and cupolas and domes arise
    In more majestic splendour than e'er gleams
In thoughts of architects or poets' eyes,
    Or palaces by painters planned in dreams.

———

All round the bright stupendous pile
　　Are terraces and gay parterres
Where fairest flowers eternal smile
　　And breathe sweet perfumes wholly theirs,
And fountains of luminous waters play
In soaring columns and spreading spray,
And drop with musical patter and plash
In purling pools where bright fish flash.

Soft zephyrs on invisible wing
Rose-fragrance with sweet music bring,
As blend the odours of the thorn,
　　The woodbine, lilac, and sweetbriar
With balmy airs of summer morn,
　　And the sweet songs of Nature's choir.

There lilies lave in limpid lakes,
　　And primulas peer where poets pass,
And snowflowers flourish without snowflakes,
　　And daffodils doze in dewless grass,
And from eternal flowering sprays
Beautiful birds trill roundelays.

He marked the splendour of the scene,
All things with ravished eyes and keen ;
With new delight his soul was filled,
His heart with newest joyance thrilled ; .

But when the Throne of Morwyn he
Saw rise beyond resplendently,
He deemed till then his senses dull
To think that aught was beautiful,
So transcendental was the blaze
Of loveliness that met his gaze !

————

I know of naught in earth or air
With that bright structure to compare,
Yet some idea might be caught
If I should say that it was wrought
More airily than cloudlet craft
That summer breezes gently waft
Between a sky serenely blue
And ocean of an azure hue.

————

Think of a white and rocky mass,
Transparent as the clearest glass,
Up from blue shining waters towering,
And from the base to summit flowering
In chaste design of sculptured bowers,
Birds, fruits, and plants, and silver showers
Of buds, and leaves luxuriant,
Through which the summer sunbeams slant
Their golden radiance.   So one may
From the creative brain convey

A semblance of the goddess' throne.
Yet lovelier far the fabric shone
Than human fancy e'er conceived,
For spangles numberless relieved
The lofty structure.   Indeed, it seemed
Built up of purest pearls that gleamed
With countless jewels all ablaze.
Inward, upward, and divers ways
Went wide white terraces with shells
And coral strown.   Three ample thrones
Were there, with coloured arcs and zones
Made marvellous; but one excels
The rest, being brighter, more ornate,
And there Morwyn in splendid state
Divinely sits; on either hand
The greatest in Earth's story stand,
The god-like Elds whose harps and arms
Were Britain's first and greatest charms.

———

This lesser throne Credwen ascends,
And lustre to its splendour lends;
In that a maiden calm and fair,
With sweet blue eyes and golden hair,
Sits silent, beautiful, serene,
Part of the glory of the scene,
And near her stands a seer whom time
Makes mystic, wonderful, sublime.

A halo bounds his silver hair
And gleams upon his lofty brow,
As sunshine in the winter bare
Enwreathes a mountain capt with snow.
His fingers stray along the strings
Of his golden harp as soft he sings;
His eye is fixed, as tranquilly
He gazed far down futurity;
His wondrous features are the while
Lit with a sweet expectant smile,
And down his breast his broad beard flows
Like an avalanche of frozen snows.

By Credwen's throne the king! How grand,
How fair, ev'n like a god! Command
Sits on his brow, and spotless truth
Dwells on his lips; eternal youth
Love lives in his blue eyes and bright;
All-perfect soldier, king, and knight,
Though king nor soldier now, for there
No arms or sway may any bear,
Where peace and rest supremely reign,
And war is not, nor hate, nor pain;
Yet at his feet a sword behold,
With jewelled hilt and sheath of gold!

Credwen left Awen at the feet
Of Morwyn, who smiled passing sweet,

And low he knelt, elate to find
Her greet him graciously and kind.
The goddess laid one pearl-white hand
Light on the minstrel's drooping head,
And, raising high her flashing wand,
In tones of wondrous music said,
"Hail, Childe from Cambrian Land! Be thine
The powers of all the immortal line!
Thine ever hence the harp shall be
To lead our Island minstrelsie.
Arise! and heed with eye and ear
What thou shalt see, what thou shalt hear."

So Awen rose, ethereal grown,
A being passing fair and bright,
The same effulgence round him thrown
As clothed those forms of joy and light.
And to him then well known became
The myriads there, by deed and name;
But first and foremost of the train
The sage and soldier, mighty twain!
He on the right was Merlyn, grand
King Arthur on the left did stand.

Then rose around a mighty song,
Led·by the Master of the throng,

And joined by Arthur's wondrous voice,
Till every soul seemed to rejoice
In one spontaneous harmony
That filled the whole immensity
Of heaven, and echoed far away,
As 'twere to Time's remotest day.

Soon as the chorus closed, the seer
On Awen smiled and drew him near.
"Behold," he said, "and listen well,
And what you mark, hereafter tell."

Intent the minstrel marked, and told
Marvels to eye and ear unrolled.
But soft! How may my muse disclose
To mortal sense such scenes as those
Which Awen wonder-wrapt reviewed?
Fain would I for a space forbear,
Nor impiously nor rashly dare
Now to recite in hasty mood,
How thwart his raptured vision passed
Long centuries, from first to last,
Those gone and some which yet may be.
Nay, pause awhile, and soon again
Methinks will come the minstrel's strain
From o'er the foaming, flashing sea.

CANTO SIXTH.

CANTO SIXTH.

When a grand river anears the grander sea,
 It moves more solemnly, more stately flows ;
No rocks or boulders mar its course, but free
 And in great majesty it onward goes.
When a great life is drawing to its close,
 The spirit is calm and passes tranquilly
From all its earthly turmoil, pains, and throes,
 And glides in grandeur imperceptibly
Into the vast unknown, deep-veiled eternity.

———

So may my song, when lighter scenes are past,
 Or grave or gay, from gay to grave return,
And in the bosom of Hereafter glassed
 May the great blaze of inspiration burn.
So shall it an immortal hearing earn
 Of those whose fates are in the future cast,
Who may in its foreshadowings discern
 That fame and glory for our land to last
Till all Earth's nations hear Creation's final blast

———

Hark !   Many mellow sounds now wake
The woods to gladness, and to take
The drowsiness of night away,
And herald the return of day.

———

The moon has set, the night withdrawn,
And grandly lifts the golden dawn ;
The mists up from the world have rolled,
The mountain-tops are crowned with gold ;
The air is full of music sweet,
Poured forth the rising sun to greet,
And over the ocean's leaping spray
Glisters many an amber ray.

———

Would that my muse might mount and sing
As mounts the lark on early wing,
That ever as he higher soars
A sweeter, wilder song downpours,
Or as the throstle on the tree
Uplifts his morning melody,
How should my soul rejoice and rise
From brightening hills to brighter skies.

———

But sweeter than the thrush's,
Intenser than the lark's,
Far lovelier than all songs that come from scented bushes
Now on the ear embarks,

As every other singer drops his head and hushes.
How it falls and flushes,
Ever rich and rare,
The most delicious music that floats along the air !

"Awen Wealh, wake !
Arise and behold
The land of your birth once more ;
See the day break
With a shimmer of gold
On the bold and beautiful shore !

" Look once again
On the land and sea,
On the hills, and the woods, and the streams ;
Call back the strain
That was sweetest to thee,
And the spot that was part of thy dreams.

"Awake ! and again
When you need repose
You shall lie in the loveliest bowers,
Where sorrow and pain
The heart never knows,
But blessings fall on you in showers."

Lo ! on yon heathery height where now
The sun bursts bright above its brow,
And in an emerald dint whence rise
Bald peaks that pierce the glowing skies,
Bathed in that flood of golden sheen,
A beauteous form by me is seen ;
A maid whose streaming tresses vie
With the great glory of the sky,
And over a slumbering youth she stands,
Fanning his face with her shining hands.

"Awen Wealh, wake !" she softly sings.
And while the name to her red lip clings,
Awen Wealh wakes, and his opening eyes
Gaze at the maiden with sweet surprise,
And scarcely he kens the face divine
Ere he cries, " Inglissa ! for ever mine."

" Inglissa ! Inglissa !" The hills all round
Repeated the name with a joyous sound.
Awen arose, and her finger-tips
Like rosebuds raised to his eager lips.
He said, " Inglissa, I heard your voice
From that far country whither rejoice
The greatand good of the early days
When the world was filled with primeval lays.

I heard your song with its mystical charm,
And my heart beat high with intense alarm
Lest you should vanish as long before,
When you quelled the strife in the castle hoar,
And I might never behold you again
In the land above or the home mundane—
Never to gaze on your face so fair,
Your sweet blue eyes and golden hair;
But Merlyn spoke in my anxious ears
Things which soon dispelled my fears.
' 'Tis Inglissa,' he said, ' whom you behold,
With eyes of blue and hair of gold;
And, Morwyn's will hereafter done,
Inglissa and Awen will be one.' "

———

" Awen," she pleaded, " oh, sing to me
Of the home of the Blessed Minstrelsie;
Faithfully tell me in spirit and word
What there you saw and felt and heard ! "

———

" Such were the words of the seer," he said,
As to a moss-covered rock he led
The fair Inglissa ; and side by side
They sat, as he to his harp applied
His rapid hands, and with joy and awe
Told what he felt and heard and saw.

———

" I saw and heard," he sang, " oh, sweet !
What makes the heart exultant beat.
I heard and saw," he said, "ah me !
What made the heart right rueful be.
I looked far back and seemed to scan
The time when first the world began,
And the earth was grand as men should know,
In pristine beauty and vernal glow ;
And peace and joy reigned everywhere,
And everything that moved was fair.
But while I viewed the primal scene,
Dimmer and duller grew its sheen,
And over the whole a shadow fell
That thousands of years could not dispel.

———

" ' The shadow of sin,' seer Merlyn said,
' Thus over the glory of Eden spread ! '

———

" Then fearful sounds through space uprose,
Dread cries and yells, and such as those
Men utter in hate and deadly strife
For power, liberty, glory, life,
And groans, and moans, and wailing cries,
And sobs, and tears, and curses, and sighs ;
And when the earth again I traced,
With crimson stains it was defaced.

———

" And Merlyn said, ' So flowed afar
The tide of devastating war ! '

" Lo ! then from the remotest east
  A surging purple flood outflowed,
    A mighty seething wave rushed forth,
And rolled and raged and ever increased
  As high and angrily it rode
O'er land and sea with threatening crest,
    Outspreading to the south and north,
And ever heading to the west.

" I turned my head, and joyfully
Beheld a grey-green sunlit sea,
And in it, gleaming like a star,
The white front of an isle afar.
Earth's jewel in the waves it seemed,
And on her bosom brightly gleamed ;
Then rose and rose and seemed to expand,
Till there lay before me a spacious land
With forests of oak and elm and beech,
Stretching as far as sight could reach ;
With here and there, of primeval green,
Plains luxuriant lying between ;
With mountains high and wide-spread vales,
Deep wooded glens and flowery dales,

Broad lakes and rivers and crystal streams
Glancing white in the bright sun's beams.

———

" A beautiful land it was, I ken,
As ever was soiled by feet of men.
I gazed upon it enwrapt awhile.
Said Merlyn, ' Britain, the Blessed Isle ! '

———

" Then from the forests of elm and oak
Sounds of the sylvan chase upbroke ;
I heard from the depths of valley and glen
The bay of hounds and shouts of men
That echoed among the hills again ;
And up and down the wild domain,
Inglissa, I saw in motley swarms,
Like fiends in foray, rude human forms
Dash hither and thither, and in and out,
With whoop and halloo, and yell and shout,
Mad and merry at once to slay
Beasts for the feast and beasts of prey.
Wild they seemed as the brutes themselves,
Fierce as demons, and jovial as elves,
Arrayed in the hides their huntings yield,
And decked with trophies of forest and field.
I looked where Merlyn had stood serene.
A change passed over the lovely scene ;

I stood alone, and I knew not where,
But still in a land exceeding fair.

—

" Feud and foray are over, and see!
Warriors and hunters on bended knee,
With heads low-bending, and all around
Reign solemn silence and peace profound,
Save that some mystical murmuring
The whispering breezes with them bring,
And flutter along all faint and low,
As it were the muttering of some slow
Deep river whose distant waters glide
In muffled volume to the ocean wide.

—

" Nearer, nearer, and ever more near,
Clearer, clearer, and ever more clear,
Now like the flow of a swelling rill
Down the smooth side of a gentle hill;
Then came a chanting so sad and sweet,
And the steady throb of falling feet,
And through the glades of a forest vast
A solemn procession slowly passed.

—

" Steadily, sturdily, sadly, and slow,
With chant and dirge they onward go,
A band of men of mystical mien
In garments of white and blue and green,

Stateliest pilgrims in solemn guise,
Sublimely calm and supremely wise,
With silvern beards and locks like snow
That free on the air like meteors flow;
With leaves of oak and mistletoe boughs
Wreathing about their ample brows;
And on their shoulders the harps whose tones
Might thrill with fire a dead king's bones.

"Solemnly, silently, on they went,
Deep on a beautiful rite intent.
On boughs of the willow that droops and weeps
As over the spot where a loved one sleeps,
I saw they carefully, tenderly bore
A human figure shrouded o'er,
And knew by the folds of the drapery
That form was of beautiful symmetry."

Inglissa raised her widened orbs,
And seemed to say with sorrowful eyes,
"Oh, the terrible sacrifice!"
But Awen, as one whose tale absorbs
Himself as well as his hearers, sped
On with his story, and further said:

"Anon they came to a lonely dell
Where dark on the sward the shadows fell

Of foliage dense of forest trees,
Waving their arms in a mournful breeze,
And tearful flowers looked up at the sun
From banks of waters that gurgling run
'Neath drooping willows and aspens frail,
'Neath gloomy yews and elders pale.

———

"There they halted with air forlorn,
And set on the sward the burden borne ;
Then, drooping, in mazy ways they trod,
Silently praying to Hu their god
And ever returned by devious way
To gaze on the form that listless lay.

———

"Meanwhile the leader of all the crowd
At the head of the prostrate figure bowed,
And slowly drew from the head to the feet
A fur pall white as a winding-sheet,
And there all prone on the grass so green
The mightiest warrior-prince was seen.

———

"The paleness of death was over his face,
And the sweat of death on his brow,
The languor of death in his eyes had place ;
It was death who had laid him low

———

" A warrior-prince and a princely bard,
Mute he lay on the soft green sward,
Dead in the morn of manhood's might,
Dead in the flush of beauty's light !

———

" Mute and motionless, cold and prone,
Like some marvel in sculptured stone
Dashed to earth by an impious hand,
In very impotence glorious, grand !

———

" Look at his limbs, huge, knotted, and bare !
What was the power that slumbered there ?
His raven locks in abandonment flow
Over his cold white cheeks and brow,
Trailing about his columned throat,
And over his massive breast to float.

———

" Still in his gripless hands he held
The axe and spear and mighty bow
With which the fiercest feud he quelled,
And vengeance dealt on many a foe ;
Still at his side the harp that knew
Him in his softer moods, and drew
Forth from his subtle brains those strains
Oft heard throughout his wide domains.

———

" Framed both to fire the moody thralls
And bold chiefs in embattled towers,.
To 'guile brave knights in festive halls
And high dames in their secret bowers.
But though those strings were hushed for ever,
And chilled for aye his heart and fingers,
His mighty name could perish never,
Nor end his songs with after-singers.
So knew those sages as they sorrowed
In triple circles round his bier,
Relief from lamentations borrowed,
And sang the praise and dropped the tear.
So knew the Arch Eld with steadfast eye
Fixed on the burning sun on high,
Who with his harp and deep voice led
This rueful requiem over the dead :

I.

" Lay aside the axe and the spear,
Come from the chase and the battle,
Come from the tops of the mountains,
Come from the depths of the forests,
For Luarch the Brave and the Good,
The princely Luarch, is dead !

II.

" Lay aside the crook and the plough,
Come from the fields and the folds,

Take up the reed and the telyn,
Come from the feasts of the mighty,
For Luarch the Noble and Wise,
Luarch the Learned, is dead !

III.

" ' Lo ! low he lies,
   Luarch the Wise,
But Luarch the Brave'
Hath conquered the grave.
Luarch the Beautiful
Hath gone like a dutiful
Son to the Palace of Blue,
To his father, Eternal Hu !

IV.

" ' Warriors shall see him no more,
Hunters shall hear him no more ;
No more he will lead in the battle,
No more in the chase he will rally ;
The tones of his harp will resound not,
We shall hear his sweet voice nevermore,
Till we sail o'er the hyaline ocean
That flows to the Blissful Shore !

V

" 'Warriors may weep for him,
Hunters may mourn for him,
Maidens may pine in their bowers,
Luarch will heed them not,
Luarch will hear them not ;
He will be walking with Tergwith !

VI.

" 'Then come with the herbs that are sweetest,
Gather the loveliest flowers,
Bring ye the boughs of the oak tree ;
The crystal mistletoe bring ye,
The leaves of the shining laurel,
Sweetbriar, whitethorn, and woodbine,
And build up the tomb of lost Luarch !'

———

" And lo ! they came from far and near,
Warriors and hunters would there appear
To chant the runes the sages wove,
And thread the mazes of glade and grove ;
To gather the beautiful herbs and flowers
That grew in the forest's untrodden bowers,
Plants and boughs of delicious perfume
For the building up of Luarch's tomb !

———

" While they chanted the tomb was made,
Spray upon spray being gently laid,
Blossom on blossom, and bough on bough,
Oak, then laurel, and mistletoe now,
Sweetbriar, myrtle, and maidenhair ferns,
Woodbine, mosses, and heather by turns;
And, to guard the pile from the beasts of prey,
They covered it over with yew and clay;
Then slowly, sadly, and sorrowing still,
Their ways retraced by valley and hill,
And homeward thence, under sun and moon,
They chanted ever this wrathful rune :

I.

" ' O crabbed, cruel, criminal Death !
Gluttonous feaster on human breath,
Slaying and gorging and hungering still,
Oh, when, dread Death, wilt thou have thy fill ?

II.

" ' Murderous Death ! thou art everywhere—
Down in the water and up in the air,
Over the land and over the sea,
There's never a spot untouched by thee.

III.

" ' There's never a place how bright or fair
But thy dark presence will enter there ;

There's never a form now blithe or gay
But thou wilt follow and make thy prey.

IV.

" ' Through greenest valleys we've seen thee steal,
Over highest hills we have tracked thy heel;
Thou strikest the greatest in all the land,
The lowliest never escapes thy hand.

V.

" ' O treacherous, stealthy, thieving Death !
Now thou hast quenched the kingliest breath,
Now thou hast stolen from Britain one
Who was Britain's heart and Britain's sun.

VI.

" ' Oh, mighty heart for Britain oft bled,
Britain's is bleeding for thee now dead ;
Oh, mighty spirit all spirits that led,
Britain's with sorrow for thee is dead ! '

———

" When ceased those tones of lamentation,
And I no more those voices heard,
A scene too brief in its duration,
But far more jubilant occurred.
I saw King Arthur in his pride,
With all his famous knights beside,

N

The centre of the noblest train
That ever graced a king's domain.
Around him all his peoples move
As stars move round the sun above,
Each glassing back the wondrous light
That made them all so pure and bright.
And there too were the bards, whose lays
The great king loved to hear and praise—
Great bards who so well loved their king,
And so his godlike acts admired,
That they could never tire to sing
The noble lays his life inspired.

" The scene was hard by Iska's stream,
Near old Caerleon's crumbled walls,
Where bright the mountain waters gleam,
And light the tide stream fills and falls.
A circled ground the hills between
Where many a famous joust had been.

" There Arthur sat in regal state,
The wisest, noblest, worthiest king,
Admired and honoured by the great,
And reverenced by the meanest thing—
Sat silent in his rock-formed chair,
As wondrous as the hills and old ;

Calm at his side Guenyver fair,
With lovely ladies she controlled.

———

" It was the time when knights and bards
Competed for the king's rewards,
And every one supremely strove
Less for the prize than Idris' love—
The knights for skill of eye and hand
In dangerous joust and high command ;
The bards for subtlest melody
That wedded words and sounds might be,
And many and stirring were the themes
They wove their glorious pæans on.
Far lovelier than are heard in dreams
Was every melody ; but one ! —
Oh, marvellous song ! Oh, song divine !
Would that thy mighty power were mine !

———

" Inglissa, list ! Hear you that strain ?
Methinks 'twill echo in my brain
For ever more. Would you could know
How grand and rapturous was its flow !

———

" It was the Bard of bards who sang !
From Merlyn's harp those raptures sprang

Respondent to the master's hand ;
Around, above, and everywhere
They thrilled the circumambient air,
    And filled with song the lovely land.

———

" Hark ! those beauteous tones ascending,
Sweetly varying, meetly blending !
Now they laugh, and now they weep,
Now they are shallow, now they are deep ;
Now they come with impetuous flow,
Now they are solemn, deep, and slow ;
Now they light the heart with gladness,
Now they dim the soul with sadness ;
Now we pity, and now we blame,
Now vengeful hate, and now love's flame
Tingles through the throbbing blood.

———

" Thus with ever-varying mood
Seemed those knightly souls bestirred,
Till a languishing wail they heard,
    As 'twere the dying of the lay.
Then they turned to Arthur's Chair ;
Lo ! the king no longer there !
    Great Merlyn, too, had passed away !
Then seemed it that the world's great light
    Had vanisht, leaving all things dark,

Till back from the mysterious flight
　There came a mystic song thus—hark !

I.

" ' Time is arch Iconoclast,
　Weaver of the triple crown,
Present, future, and the past,
　Builder up, and puller down !
Ask not what these things portend ;
Time to all things brings an end.

II.

" ' Brightest days must close full soon,
　Sweetest seasons soon decline,
Summer's sun and winter's moon,
　Autumn mellow, vernal shine.
Ask not what these things portend ;
Time to all things brings an end.

III.

" ' Kingliest king, and knightliest knight,
　Even the greatest of his kind,
People, power, glory, and might,
　All these now must leave behind.
Ask not what these things portend ;
Time to all things brings an end.'

" And still the far-off echoes long
Repeat the burden of the song :
' Oh, ask not what these things portend ;
Time to all things will bring an end.' "

————

Then Awen paused, and poignant grief
In wild tears found a brief relief.
To deepest anguish moved he wept,
While his wandering fingers swept
His harp-strings over, making wail
Those sounding to the saddest tale.

————

Death-white Inglissa's cheeks had grown,
Her fear-fraught eyes o'erflowed with tears ;
In pleading ways her arms were thrown,
She strove to soothe away his fears.

————

It was in vain she sought to know
The cause of Awen's mental throe.
No words his burning lips could find
To tell the bodings in his mind,
And all despairingly she pressed
Her head upon his heaving breast.
Then lo ! as if she'd touched the spring
Of his racked heart's great sorrowing,

Fast from his lips began to flow
Unbid, unchecked, this tale of woe :

———

" Oh, break my heart ! burst forth, my soul !
Or I must evermore sing dole.
Oh, eyes, see not, be deaf my ears,
Ere such a scene again appears.
Be silent, harp, be mute, O tongue,
Nor evermore give voice to song,
Lest the vast universe should be
Thrilled with the direst threnody.

———

"Scarce had the master's wrathful lay
Died on the wind of time away,
And hardly had the mighty twain
Evanished from the knightly train,
Ere darkling down the sunlit sea
Rode War's foul wave resistlessly,
And then I knew that song's portent
That knelling through the Island went.

———

" Again wild war-cries filled the air,
And bands of warriors everywhere
In haste appear, and downward pour
To where the white waves sweep the shore—
White now, but all too soon, I know,
Red with the blood of men to flow,

The life-blood of a noble band,
Shed for the love of native land !

———

" Nearer, nearer, the war-wave came,
Bearing legions with helms aflame,
And spears that gleam in golden rays
On land and rolling sea which blaze.
Ah ! like the sea methought the host
That bore down on the crowded coast
And like the coast the warrior band
That fearless waited on the land.
The sea will sway and still will roll
Persistent to its destined goal ;
The shore's defiant, but the sea
Triumphant evermore will be.
Ah ! mighty was the chief on sea,
And mighty, too, the chief on land,
But this one warred 'gainst destiny,
And that smote with a victor's hand !

———

" Near, still nearer the war-wave came,
Spear and battle-axe flash and flame ;
The hosts on land, the hosts on sea
Were brave and proud as hosts may be.

———

" Then as from distant mountain caves
Down on the shore-borne crested waves
New-loosened blasts will fiercely sweep
And lash to fury all the deep ;
As mighty waters meet and rear
Their white steeds in the foam-filled air ;—
So those fierce hostile forces met
Ere yet a foot on shore was set,
Before a keel had struck the sands
That bound the Isle with golden bands.
And soon the white-maned waves were red
With blood for Eagle and Dragon shed ;
And soon the land, all green before,
Was purple-sodden with mingled gore,
Sheer to the heights from the red shore,
And the Eagle triumphed more and more.

" Far over the Isle the red flood flowed,
And lake and river all crimson glowed,
But its waves were shattered in many a shock,
As the sea is broken by many a rock
And backward hurled ere finally
It rolls in might and majesty
O'er everything that barred its course.

" War-waves went over the land perforce,
And ah ! no more that Isle was bright,
For Conquest dimmed its pristine light,
And over its face a darkness spread
Like a funeral pall thrown over the dead.
As carrion birds descend to feed
On the fallen corse of noblest steed,
So swept the ravenous nations down
To prey on the hero-land overthrown.

" There hosts and hosts still came and sped,
And blood on blood was ever shed,
Till Time had notched on the mundane tree
Many a fearful century,
And deeply carved on branch and bole
Records of deeds to shame man's soul.
Yet ever with hand unwearied, and heart
Unblenched, the Men of the Isle would part
With life's last spasm rather than be
Befouled with the brand of slavery.

" Anon another and beautiful change
Passed over the Wiht Land's seabound range.
As morning mists all dense and dun
Uplift before the approaching sun,
So rose the darkness from that Isle,
And was dispelled till a sunny smile

Irradiated from sea to sea,
Heralding peace and purity,
And the land was bright from shore to shore,
As raindrops glisten when storms are o'er.

———

" Inglissa, once I stood again
In sight of the mysterious train,
And thought more luminous and grand
Seemed mighty Morwyn's glorious band,
And even Merlyn's face methought
A greater glory still had caught ;
And straightway every voice and heart
Was thrilled with some harmonious part
That blent with others, and then combined
Rose in one strain vast as the wind :—

———

" ' Fallen are Britain's enemies
Beneath the dust of centuries,
But free is Britain evermore,
One mighty land from shore to shore ;
And hence her sons, with joy and pride,
Will Freedom's flag bear side by side
Through every land and every clime,
Throughout the world, and through all time.

———

    "'Her peoples ever forth shall speed
To spread the liberty they know,
And on the lands they light and lead
The sun shall never cease to glow.
Then shall King Arthur come again
To reassume his godlike reign,
And all his faithful knights and true
Shall form the Table Round anew,
And Britain, fairer grown and greater,
Shall praise his mightier reign and later.'

"Lo! Arthur smiled, and with benignant eye
Looked on the land that bright'ning still did lie
Purged of all blemish in the purple sea,
Fit home of heroes, love, and chivalry.
But though the glamour of that glorious smile
Heightened the splendour of the lustrous Isle,
Gone from my gaze again that face serene,
Gone from my vision that resplendent scene.
Yet in my ears the singers' voices sound,
Linger their tones above and all around.
Then in the west uprose a mighty form,
Dark'ning the sky as 'twere a rising storm;
Far to the east his awful shadow spread,
And thus the Spirit of the Mountains said:

" ' I yield them up, and bid them speed,
　O'er Britain's blood-washed land ;
My saving care no more they need,
　Nor my avenging hand.
Long centuries mid looming rocks
　I've sheltered them, and broke
Malignant war's persistent shocks
　And slavery's ruthless yoke.
I welcomed them when sorely pressed
　By fierce invading hordes,
And with my adamantine breast
　Turned Hate's relentless swords.
But now when peace is over all,
　And men more human grown,
I yield them up to Freedom's call,
　Who'll give them back their own.
Up, then, brave sons of Britain's Isle !
　My mountains no more bar
You from fair plains that eastward smile,
　Nor Conquest's blood-red car.'

Calmly the Mountain Spirit then descended
Upon a sun-bathed summit, and extended
His huge form downward on the sun-warmed side,
As some great being whose chiefest work is ended
Takes rest well earned with quietude allied,
While on his forehead peace with glory blended,

And his whole form was smoothed and beautified.
Then from the sea a luring voice upcried :

———

" ' Unloose your winds, eternal hills,
 To lash my sluggish tide,
And I will bear their stately ships
 Where any ships may ride.
I'll make these Islesmen rulers sole
 Of every curbless wave,
And every land shall own their sway,
 Yet no land own a slave.'

———

" For a brief period I could plainly see
Queenly Naiada posing gracefully
Above the shining waves, her tresses bright
Streaming all ways afar like tracks of light
Along the trackless waters, one dimpled hand
Was resting on an anchor, a coral wand
Magnetic in the other gleamed and quivered.
Some silent, gladsome message this delivered
To all the hill-born streams, for straight each one
With fuller, faster flow began to run,
And sing, ' We'll seek their stately ships, O sea,
And bear them swiftly, proudly down to thee."

———

" Then from far Deva's holy flood
    The voice of Arfen came,
Who ever fired the Briton's blood
    With patriotism's flame.
' Go forth,' she said, ' ye noble ones,
    And let the world be free ;
Ye were the first of Britain's sons,
    First too of Liberty.
Then meet it is that ye should bear
    The banner now unfurled,
Proclaiming progress everywhere,
    And peace throughout the World ! '

———

" Lo ! like the fabled birds that spring
From their own ashes, triumphing
Over Death and his sleuth serf Decay,
They came from Cambrian Hills away,
And once again the Wiht Land teemed
With strident souls whom some men deemed
Long and for aye exterminated.
All the land was stirring as 'twere fated
For some vast enterprise.   Then you,
Inglissa, on my raptured view
Again burst forth !   Your longed-for voice
Made my heart dance, my soul rejoice.

You called me, who with burning brain
So long had sought you, and in vain.
Nay, I had deemed you lost.   Poor heart,
To be so weak !   But now we part
No more.   Inglissa, hark ! that hymn
Sung as it were by seraphim :
' Heart to heart in endless unity,
And soul to soul.'   Oh, ecstasy ! "

———

So Awen's wondrous tale was done.
That moment, too, the brightest sun
Of all the year shone forth, yet sheer
Darkness it was beside the clear
Light flashed those forms around.   It dazed
My senses.

———

   When again I raised
My darkened eyes, I could but see
An old man and a maiden.   She
Gladysa was, Syr Utar he.
Then loomed old Garif in their wake,
With him a motley band to take
Their master to his Towers again.
Their search had been sore, long, and keen,
But nowhere they had Awen seen.
Yet all in one direction strain,

As if they marked with awful gaze
Above the height that marvellous blaze,
And still with keen and curious eye
Kept careful watch on hill and sky.

———

With tottering steps and head low bent,
Utar assayed the steep ascent,
And at his side with weary feet,
But still with cheery voice and sweet,
Gladysa walked and strove in vain
His drooping figure to sustain ;
Her tender efforts all despite,
That new-born day brought him death's night.

———

A resting-place at last was gained ;
The old knight's eyes were upward strained,
The feeble feet no further went,
The weary head was lower bent.
" No more, no more ! " the white lips gasped,
" No more ! " the trembling fingers clasped ;
More heavily he pressed her arm.
Gladysa heard with dire alarm
These muttered words : " Oh, false or true !
No more his face my eyes shall view ;
If he be false, alive or dead,
My curses on his alien head !

o

If true—ay, true as it must be—
Heaven shower its blessings, boy, on thee !"

———

No more he spoke ; his latest word
His faithful daughter then had heard,
And knew no more.   O'erspent at length
Her woman's and affection's strength,
She swooned, but timely to her aid
Came Garif and her serving-maid.
With hands claspt upwards, and with eyes
Turned darkening from the bright'ning skies,
Fell Utar forward, pulseless, dead,
Green pillow for his snowy head.

———

And Awen Wealh no more was seen
Among the hills and valleys green ;
But from the lonely haunts of sound,
That towering beacon's height around,
Were heard the echoes of a voice
To make the hearts of men rejoice,
And on a fearful ledge on high,
O'erhanging in the middle sky
Where human foot may never tread,
A youthful form recumbent, dead !
There to remain perchance for aye,
For to it none could find a way.

———

Deep was Gladysa's grief, and dire
Her woe and wail above her sire,
And Garif and the servitors
Lent lamentations loud to hers ;
But through the glory of the morn
Meantime sweet melodies were borne,
And though no singer there they saw
'Twas Credwen's song they heard with awe.

———

"Sire and scion have passed away,
But only the one shall know decay.
Lay Syr Utar's ashes to rest
Under the mountain's rugged crest ;
Rugged the thoughts were in his brain,
Rugged the heart now silent lain !

———

" Awen the minstrel's life is long
In a sweet unquenchable song
Given to gladden the world always,
That loves delicious untraceable lays,
Showing the power of song is wrought
Out of the hidden, spiritual thought,
And brighter, grander, holier glows
When free from earthly and fleshly throes.

———

" Bury Syr Utar under the hill ;
  Howl, O winds, his funeral dirge !
The spirit was stormy that now is still ;
  Roll, O sea, your sonorous surge !

" Men and manners and customs change ;
  Sing, O birds, your dolorous lays !
The wildest life hath the shortest range ;
  Rave, O rills, in sinuous ways !

" Lay his head on a pillow of grass ;
  Wave, O trees, your shadowy arms !
Write his name on a tablet of brass ;
  Ravens, croak your ghostly alarms !

" Utar will rest in the lone hill-side,
The winds may howl, and boom the tide,
The rills will run in meandering courses,
The woods be swayed by Æolian forces,
The birds will whistle or sadly or gay,
Ravens will croak while the lambkins play,
But good Gladysa shall live to hear
A voice on earth that shall have no peer,
And know the land of her ancestrie
The centre of song again to be."

AFTERTONES.

HYMN OF UNITY.

So was my seeing ended, but as those last tones fell,
Faint but yet distinctly on my hearing seemed to swell
The sounds of noble music, as above the city's din
One hears from a cathedral the festival within.
It was the hymn of unity resounding far and wide,
And it told of radiant spirits for ever unified ;
The bridal of great harmonies, assimilated minds,
The confluence of affinities, and welding of best kinds,
The blending of vast cadences, the grouping of sweet
    sounds,
Through space's farthest reaches and time's remotest
    bounds.

THE HYMN TRIUMPHAL.

I heard the hymn triumphal,
    The Merlyn's master strain ;
The voices heard of Morwyn,
    King Arthur, and their train.

MORWYN.

By my sway on land, on the unfathomed sea,
By the joy of song, the power of poesy,

By the might of Right, the right of Liberty,
   Hear me, future bards and sages,
   Hear me, all ye unborn ages,
   With solemnity declare,
   And with due, undying care
   Hence these chosen twain shall be—
   Awen Wealh the minstrel he,
   And the fair Inglissa she—
   Joined in endless unity.

Many Voices.

   We hear thee, O Morwyn !
   And greatly rejoice ;
   Thy wish is our pleasure,
   Thy choosing our choice !

MERLYN.

By our love for thee, Morwyn,
   Guide and glory, star and queen ;
By my own divining e'en ;
By the sacred fire that gleams
Quenchless in my prescient dreams ;
By my love for that brave race
Whom I left on Britain's face,
By the bliss their souls shall know,
Ending turmoil, war, and woe ;—
Hear me, all ye greatest singers,

Earliest and latest singers,
Thus declare these twain are one—
Awen Wealh the minstrel he,
And the fair Inglissa she—
Till the quenching of the sun,
Till the sands of time run dry,
Till sad death himself shall die !

Many Voices.

We hear thee, O Merlyn !
And greatly rejoice ;
Thy word is our compact,
Thy choosing our choice.

ARTHUR.

By the bliss my soul hath known
In the light of Morwyn's throne,
While uncounted time hath flown ;
By the glory yet to be ;
By the joy to them and me,
When I go to dwell again
With them in the loved domain,
In the Blessed Isle and great
Where my deep-loved people wait,
Hear me, O my knights so fair,
Hear me Bards and Sages there,
By my Table Round declare,

This loved union which I bless—
Awen Wealh the minstrel he
And the Rose of England she—
Is a triumph, and no less
Than the doom of heathenness !
Hence my Table shall be found
Compassing the world around,
And our people wandering free
Through the world in unity,
While their swelling songs will soar
In sweet accordance evermore !

Many Voices.

We hear thee, great Arthur,
Chief King and chief Knight ;
Thy hope is our anchor,
Thy seeing our sight !

CONCLUSION.

As when the doors of the cathedral close,
We hear the voices of the choir no more ;
As when the wind from a new quarter blows,
Bearing from us the sounds to us it bore ;—
So ceased, far passing, on my ear to fall
The sounds of that celestial festival.

O TERRIBLY TURBULENT SEA!

ROLL, swirl, and seethe,
  O terribly turbulent sea !
Wash, boom, and hurl
  . Thy white-winged waves over me.
Thy salt spray's on my lips,
  Thy breath on my icy brow,
Thy song moans through my brain,
  My singing is ended now.
My time is past, and so
  One only favour I crave—
That thou will roll and make,
  With shingle and weed my grave.
A greater song than mine
  Will drop on thy breakers yet,
A song so great the world
  Will never again forget.
All songs that have been sung
  Must seem mere jingle to this,
Will ring through the earth when I
  Am wrapt in eternal bliss.

HARK! THE SONGS OF JUBILEE.

HARK! now what sounds are rising
　From Britain's Isles once more;
What voices those resounding
　On earth's remotest shore?
What is that vast rejoicing,
　What may that gladness mean?
A thousand peoples glory
　In the reign of Britain's Queen.

———

Queen and Empress too is she,
Queen for half a centurie

———

Supreme above all nations
　The Isle of Britain stands;
Supreme spreads Greater Britain
　O'er many mighty lands.
God save the glorious empire,
　God save the Empress Queen;

Send Britain's rule for ever
   Pure, peaceful, and serene!

———

Hark! the songs of Jubilee
Over every land and sea!

O MEN WHO LEAD IN THE LAND!

O MEN who lead in the land of lands
　　That leads all lands of the earth,
Gauge right the mighty trust in your hands,
　　And grow in greatness of worth.
Behold in Britain a spreading tree,
　　With roots in the deep sea sunk,
Whose round the range of the world will be,
　　Foliage, branches, and trunk.
Foster the furthermost twigs and sprays
　　As jealous you guard the bole ;
The fruit of your work will be always
　　The pride and strength of the whole.
But let one limb be unheeded lopped,
　　And people unborn will rue
The fall of the mighty oak o'ertopped
　　That out of the deep sea grew.
So hath the ancient Aneurin sung,
　　And so it shall surely be,
Else why the heart of the Poet rung,
　　Else wherefore should Seer see ?

OTHER PIECES.

IN THE PRIME OF GOLDEN SUMMER.

In the prime of golden summer,
  A new-comer
Glad I welcomed to my bosom,
  Tiny blossom!

A bright flower of wondrous sweetness
  And completeness,
And I said, " With strong endeavour
  I for ever
This sweet bud will guard and cherish,
  Ne'er to perish
Till I fail of my endeavour—
  Then or never!

White that flower, and pure and holy,
  Spotless wholly,
But within the petals folded,
  Perfect moulded,
I beheld a lovely creature
  Whose each feature

Seemed a light from heaven descended,
    Softly blended.
Like all lights from skyward riven,
    And God-given—
Pink cheeks dimpled, eyes serenely
    Blue and queenly !   .

———

Such a God-wrought, living statue
    Looking at you,
With her blue eyes' deep profoundness,
    Rendered groundless
All your hopes of joy without her ;
    And about her—
As blue heaven about the earth is,
    Joy round mirth is—
Was all love, light, life, and glory !
    À priori
You would closer to your bosom
    Press that blossom.

———

So I pressed it ever nearer,
    Ever dearer,
Saying, " Winter storms come snarling,
    O my darling !
But I'll closer press and shield you—
    Never yield you

To his clutches.   Then instanter
The enchanter,
Death and Winter stalked together
O'er the heather,
And despite each fond endeavour,
· I shall never
Clasp again that blue-eyed blossom
To my bosom.

AS CHILDREN PLAY IN CHURCH-YARDS

ONCE more the lovely spring is come !   Again
　　She decks the landscape—woods, plains, and hills—
　　With fresh verdure and young flowers, and fills
The air with balm and many a wild bird's strain.

No more the world is drear ; no more the earth
　　Is cold and mute, wrapt in her shroud of snow.
　　Glad nature casts aside her garb of woe,
And leaps up radiant with new life and mirth.   ·

Robed in new glory comes the sun at morn,
　　And fills with light and grace and love anew
　　All things below.   With clearer, brighter blue
The sky is spread, and smiles on earth new-born.

Dread Death is powerful, but life is brave
　　And quick, and ever changing, ever new.
　　As children play in churchyards, so we view
The young life laugh above the old life's grave.

THE DANE'S DEATH.

A LEGEND OF WORCESTER CATHEDRAL.

LONG ages past, in fierce marauding days,
  When Britain's shores with Danish soldiers swarmed,
And wild Norse sagas swelled with Vikings' praise,
  And scorn of those who fled their might alarmed,

A hardy host of Denmark's daring bands
  Plied oar and sail far up the Severn Sea,
Gazing with greed on those fair fertile lands
  From either shore that sloped delightfully.

A goodly band in pride of war arrayed,
  In conscious might and arms of shining steel,
With golden beards on ample breasts displayed,
  And hearts beneath no clemency to feel.

But one there was by softer feelings moved
  Than those which urged his comrades in the fight;
A maiden fair in the North Land he loved,
  Her voice his music and her eyes his light.

One amber ringlet on his heart lay pressed,
   Her eyes' pure blue seemed all above him spread,
And as his stalwart form plied for the West,
   His love-borne spirit back to Denmark sped.

For her and Denmark he would fearlessly
   Fierce wars for plunder and adventure wage,
Seek prize and trophy over land and sea,
   Nor pause the laws of right or ruth to gauge.

Thus far in concord with that host he was ;
   And all stemmed stealthily the inland tide
Till under ancient Worcester's walls they pause,
   A famous city then by Severn's side.

Their boats made fast, to shore they lightly leapt,
   And softly, swiftly through the city sped,
As by surprise from their defences swept,
   The citizens in transient terror fled.

Havoc and pillage soon the Danes began,
   And sacked the city of its treasure store ;
Then all save one back to their barges ran,
   And down Sabrina's stream their booty bore.

Back to the city stream the populace,
  When passed the panic of their swift surprise;
And as the ruthless ravages they trace,
  Vow vengeance deep on vanished enemies.

The Danes were gone! The citizens in vain
  Rushed on, enraged revenge to wreak, and wrest
Their treasured wealth from the foe's grasp again;
  Then some to the cathedral hotly pressed.

There eagerly his secret search to urge,
  One Dane alone of all that band remained,
And from the fane behold him now emerge,
  Bearing a prize at last too dearly gained.

In the North Land in vain a maiden fair
  Waited and watched for one who came no more;
Alive they flayed him on that sacred stair,
  And nailed his skin to the cathedral door!

A thousand years into the past had slipped,
  And mouldered doors had given place to new,
An antiquary, groping in the crypt,
  Found an old board, which to the light he drew.

There still it clung, that once fair human hide,
   'Gainst which perchance her cheek was often pressed,
'Neath which once beat a heart all fears defied—
   It glowed athwart a leal, love-laden breast !

Who journeys to the " Faithful City " may
   See the grim relic of those barbarous times,
Long tanned by Time, impervious to decay,
   And hear the legend woven in these rhymes.

A FLOWER OF THE FANCY.

THERE are flowers of the fancy,
　　There are blooms that live and die,
There are blossoms that we see not,
　　But may gaze on by-and-by.
In the shimmer after showers,
　　In the summer's golden shine,
I have watched wee flowers blowing,
　　Passing beautiful, divine.

———

There was one I fondly cherished—
　　Oh, it was so fair and sweet!
Just a modest little blossom,
　　But so perfect and complete.
Gazing on its outward whiteness,
　　I perceived its hidden grace ;
Saw within a seraph spirit,
　　Saw a rose-pink, dimpled face—

———

Rose-pink limbs so sweetly moulded,
　　Finger-tips of rosy hue,
Fairy tresses, silken lashes,
　　Rosebud mouth, and eyes of blue.
Gazing down those eyes' blue dream-worlds,
　　" I will shield you with my life
From the bleaching blasts of winter,
　　From the world's disastrous strife ! "

———

Saying thus, I looked a moment
　　To the flow'rs on either side,
When that instant came the reaper
　　Of all flowers, and it died ;
Came a blast from deepest winter,
　　Came a cloud of whitest snow,
And my blossom passed for ever
　　To where blooms immortal blow.

THE LEGEND OF WORCESTER CATHEDRAL.

(ANOTHER VERSION.)

PART I.

THE day was dark for England,
  Though cloudless was the sun ;
It was by Danish soldiers
  Despoiled and overrun.
Wild swelled the fierce Norse sagas
  With deeds by Vikings done.

———

Arrayed in pride of battle,
  Elate with victory,
A band of daring Norsemen
  Sailed up the Severn Sea ;
Brave Sweyn, with breast love-riven,
  Was of the company.

———

They saw the red sun rising
  O'er Bredon's wooded height,

They marked the same sun sinking
  Behind the Malverns bright;
Helm, oar, and sail lay idle
  Till passed the silent night.

———

Not yet the lark hath risen
  To greet the dawn with song,
As past the groves of Kempsey
  They lightly skim along;
Sweet dreams of gifts for Gretchen
  In Sweyn's love-fancies throng.

———

Grand was the summer morning
  O'er old Vigornia spread,
Clear-glassed the noble Severn
  The blue sky overhead:
The ancient city echoed
  With hurried martial tread.

———

"The Danes are in the city!"
  Loud cried the frenzied folk.
"Let no Dane reach the river?"
  The city captain spoke;
Fierce oaths of direst vengeance
  From all the people broke.

PART II.

The Danes their craft are plying
  By Teme's mouth distantly,
Fair winds and flowing waters
  Bear them towards the sea.
They count their shares of plunder,
  But Sweyn, lo! where is he?

By Rhydd the boats speed downward,
  'Twere death to hesitate.
In vain that fair Norse maiden
  For Sweyn must watch and wait;
His heart's blood forth is rushing
  By yon cathedral gate.

A thousand years or nearly
  Into the past has slipt,
When one went darkly groping
  In the cathedral crypt;
What was the cumbrous object
  O'er which he nearly tript?

A door antique and crumbling
  Against the dark crypt side,

And to it still was clinging
    A piece of human hide;
Still in the House of Chapter
    The fact is verified.

———

Thus ends the dreadful legend.
    Too late the eager Sweyn
Found that his daring comrades
    Had fled to boat again;
He stood in the cathedral
    A solitary Dane!

———

Stood rapt at the high altar
    In sacrilegious spell;
To him the golden vessels
    No Christian tale could tell—
His heathen hand uplifted
    Had rung the Sanctus bell!

———

In rushed the furious townsfolk
    And soldiers by the score;
They seized the laggard Norseman
    And from his quick flesh tore
The skin, and nailed it quiv'ring
    To the cathedral door!

———

God save us from such vengeance,
  Such suffering and woe,
And may our maidens never
  Fair Gretchen's anguish know,
Far in the wild Norse region
  Ten centuries ago!

THE END.

PRINTED BY WILLIAM CLOWES AND SONS, LIMITED, LONDON AND BECCLES.

CPSIA information can be obtained
at www.ICGtesting.com
Printed in the USA
BVOW03*1448270917

496095BV00008B/300/P